Countdown
By Steve Wunsch

Countdown Update 6/14/16

Senseless Acts

"A senseless act," said CNBC's Andrew Ross Sorkin speaking the morning after the March 22 terrorist attacks in Brussels. The term has been used thousands of times since 9/11, and will be used thousands more because we are solidly on track to lose the War on Terror, which will generate an endless string of such "senseless" acts. I start here with this update to my 2001 book, *Countdown*, the writing of which straddled 9/11, because these acts are anything but senseless to their perpetrators, for whom they are the most meaningful events in their lives. That we so misunderstand our enemy and our own motivations is the reason we are losing this war, as I warned we would a week after 9/11 on page one of this book.

This insight predated the war in Afghanistan, the war in Iraq, the renewed war in Afghanistan, the renewed war in Iraq, our disastrous failed attempts to extricate ourselves from either of these quagmires, and our failed adventures in Syria, Libya and many other places whose failures were also predictable and virtually predicted here, obvious on day one of the War on Terror. Not only has the world become because of our efforts far more dangerous for the people we ostensibly set out to help, our efforts have vastly increased the danger to America and Americans, as I predicted they would.

The essence of our error is that we have abandoned the principle of freedom that made America a great nation. Instead, and in direct contradiction to it, we are foisting unwelcome and un-American policies on our own people, thereby destroying jobs, wages and the American dream of a better life for our children. Worse yet, those same policies applied abroad are causing the mostly Muslim backlash against us with its senseless terrorist acts. This is what I described in this book in 2001 and then further articulated in three more books: *War On Wealth* (2011); *Nature's God* (2012); and *Life, Liberty and the pursuit of Inequality* (2015).

What is the policy error that is leading to the destruction of America from within and without? It is the modern belief that discrimination is an evil that must be eradicated, along with all of its synonyms and descendents: bias, prejudice, bigotry, stereotyping, profiling, racism, sexism, homophobia, etc. I will explain shortly why I call this a "modern" belief, one that was nowhere to be seen at America's founding. But the key point here is that the attempt to ban discrimination is actually the main cause of the divisive rancor the policy is meant to address. The reality is that this policy breeds hatred.

Four days after the Brussels attacks, Georgia Governor Nathan Deal vetoed his state's attempt at one of these popular new "religious liberty" laws, which try to use the First Amendment to block some element of the gay rights agenda. The idea is that someone opposed to gay rights, gay marriage, LGBT rights, LGBTQ rights, LGBTQI rights, etc., can use the First Amendment to protect himself legally if he refuses to bake a cake for a gay wedding, say, or a community can protect its citizens from having to allow biological men who believe they are women from entering women's restrooms. The details are unimportant, as is the fact that there are many iterations of this same basic issue. What is important is that the First Amendment has become a thin reed when it comes to protecting these rights of discrimination, which were general, broad and unquestioned at the founding of America.

But today, whether it is the Supreme Court's tortured prevarication in favor of gay marriage ("equal dignity"), or the boycotts threatened by LGBT advocates, religious liberty is going down in flames, as most of Hollywood, Silicon Valley, industrial America, blue state governments, the U.S. Justice Department and The Boss, Bruce Springsteen, have lined up against this form of freedom.

When Springsteen canceled a concert in Greensboro, North Carolina to protest that state's new "bathroom law" requiring people to use the bathrooms that correspond to the sex listed on their birth certificates, the LGBT community was up in arms. The Boss, in solidarity with that community, explained himself this way:

> To my mind, it's an attempt by people who cannot stand the progress our country has made in recognizing the human rights of all of our citizens to overturn that progress. Taking all of this into account, I feel that this is a time for me and the band to show solidarity for those freedom fighters. As a result, and with deepest apologies to our dedicated fans in Greensboro, we have canceled our show scheduled for Sunday, April 10th. Some things are more important than a rock show, and this fight against prejudice and bigotry—which is happening as I write—is one of them.

However annoyed his 15,000 fans who had tickets were (who were eligible for refunds), many in the entertainment elite immediately applauded Springsteen's move.

So what's wrong with that? Aren't those homophobes in North Carolina and other states on the wrong side of history? Isn't it a good thing that leaders in industry, government and the arts show us the way? Doesn't everyone realize that fairness for transgenders requires a new interpretation of the Constitution, as if it were a "living" document? Isn't this what America is all about? Well, yes, it certainly is what America has been all about in recent times, as we have progressively banned bias against people who belong to certain groups, such as immigrants, African Americans, women, and increasingly homosexuals or even criminals. It is now standard U.S. policy to protect people in these and many other groups from discrimination in such areas as education, employment, housing and many other aspects of life.

But this is not the way it was at the founding of America.

In the 1790s when the precursor to the New York Stock Exchange formed, the founders were able to structure their exchange and select its members in any way they saw fit. There were no restrictions on their ability to discriminate freely as they set up their exchange, which enabled them to establish the monopoly paradigm at the heart of America's capacity to create wealth. As I describe in all my books, and in detail in Life, *Liberty and the pursuit of Inequality*, this right to discriminate and set up monopolies, starting with the exchange that became the Big Board, was the secret to our success. Without it, we would never have become a wealthy or powerful nation.

As important as the right to discriminate was, perhaps equally important was the fact that there was no need to invoke any legal protections in order to exercise or claim that right, such as the Constitution, the Bill of Rights or the First Amendment, much less any special reaffirmations of those rights, such as religious liberty laws or bathroom laws. The history of the NYSE's formation mentions no legal skirmishes that were necessary to establish the exchange's and its members' right to discriminate; it's just the way it was.

Contrast that with today, where even after invoking the religious freedom supposedly embedded in the First Amendment, Americans are discovering that they have no ability anymore to discriminate in a way the Founders would have assumed was permissible and, if asked, would have insisted on. We are so used to the boilerplate describing where discrimination is illegal—national origin, religion, race, sex, etc.—that we cannot imagine that at the founding of America you could discriminate for any of those reasons, or for no reason at all, or were just plain bigoted.

But now even the believers in the bathroom bills are reduced to promoting them under the pretense that they are really only worried about *fraudulent* transgenders, i.e., heterosexual men who would use the excuse to pick their bathroom as a trick to get into the women's bathroom in order to prey on women or girls. Whether this is a real risk or just an excuse for an anti-gay law is immaterial. What is material is how circumscribed the claimed right to discriminate is, and how weak the supposed constitutional argument on which it rests is. This means that even ardent believers in these religious liberty laws do not believe they have a right to be bigoted unless their bigotry can be framed as a requirement of their religion. So even in the unlikely event that the Supreme Court ever upholds any of these religious liberty laws, that would still leave the Americans of today far less free to discriminate than early Americans were.

But back to those senseless acts. As frustrating and socially debilitating as the loss of the freedom to discriminate is in the splintering realms of sexual politics, where a new gender preference in need of protection from discrimination is seemingly discovered every other day, there are much bigger problems than this one. There are areas where blocking the right to discriminate is not just confusing or amusing, it is deadly. There are areas where attempting to eliminate the right to discriminate is already killing many people, including Americans, areas where America's antidiscrimination jihad could ultimately threaten America's very existence as well as that of many other nations. From the murder of nine worshippers in a Charleston church, to that of two New York cops having lunch in their squad car, to the killing of 77 mostly teenage children in Norway, to the slaughter of dozens, hundreds or thousands in New York, Washington, Oklahoma City, London, Paris, San Bernardino, Brussels and many other places: Every one of these murderous and mostly suicidal acts seems senseless only if you assume that the elimination of discrimination is a good idea.

If on the other hand you listen to the perpetrators themselves, it is clear that they too are taking sides in the antidiscrimination jihad. Their acts are not senseless to them because, however extreme, they are at bottom expressions of the conventional wisdom on discrimination. Even the most obviously deranged, such as the Aurora movie theater murderer, the Sandy Hook children murderer, or Norway's methodical murderer of

77 mostly teens, they see themselves as standing up for their own right to make choices, the more discriminatory and antisocial, the better. Whether or not they pursue insanity defenses at trial, they are clearly defending their own right to violent agency against government's suppression of it, their own right to dress up in commando garb and play out their antigovernment fantasy by making a show of killing exactly those the government and public think they have the least right to kill. As one chronicler of Norway's killer put it, they are saying, "Look at me, look at me!" as I do just what you tell me I can't do. By taking its antidiscrimination positions, government gives all of them a reason to think and act as they do. In a society where The Boss can see LGBT defenders as "freedom fighters," these killers can see themselves as freedom fighters, too, and it is a pose that fits conventional wisdom like a glove. When taking sides in the political battles and "national conversations" of the day is what you're *supposed* to do, even killers can think they are sacrificing themselves for freedom no matter which side they are on.

As the arguments become more contentious and the demonstrations more violent, the most fervent believers seek immortality and the respect of their fellows via suicide selfies on Facebook, Twitter and YouTube linked to lengthy manifestoes, books and statements intended to incite conflict, revolution or race wars. Whether the perpetrator is from one of the traditional discriminated against groups or its opponents, either way he sees himself as adopting and acting on political views that are not too far from the mainstream, however over-the-top the senseless act is. And so he fantasizes about what he will do, taking as much care as he can to plan the final scene and act of his life where he will be the star, a selfless hero given maximum coverage for his sacrifice by press and police reports that will record the importance of his existence for all time.

Virtually every controversial cause that fills the front pages or results in demonstrations around the world can be seen through this lens: women's rights, gay rights, Black Lives Matter, the Confederate Flag, immigration, inequality, Occupy Wall Street, health care, education, austerity, Greece, girls education, pre-K, affordable housing, girls education in Afghanistan, girls education in Pakistan, women driving in Saudi Arabia, Syrian war refugees, Muslim terrorism, suicide bombings, Sunnis versus Shiites versus Kurds, Charlie Hebdo, Je Suis Charlie, Je Suis Muslim. All are tied to causes that seek to address unfairness by eliminating discrimination or compensating for its unfair consequences via redistribution. It is because politicians promote these group-based causes that the senseless act perpetrators can imagine they are acting bravely and honorably, that they are doing something selfless and good on their way out.

When President Obama in his Amazing Grace eulogy after the Emanuel 9 murders in Charleston dwells on the persistent lack of economic progress for African Americans in spite of many redistributive policies meant to benefit them, or when Supreme Court justices allow affirmative actions that favor blacks over whites for the same reason, we should not be surprised at either the audience in Charleston loudly agreeing with the president, or that fringe actors from both of the affected groups might imagine that violence against the other group will be cheered by at least some in their own group. We should not be surprised that a Dylann Roof, after picturing himself with guns and Confederate Flags on Facebook, would murder those blacks in that bible class, or that Ismaaiyl Brinsley, after watching anti-cop demonstrations after Ferguson, would tell bystanders "Watch what I'm going to do" before shooting those cops eating lunch in their squad car. The atrocities, the senseless acts, are in all cases just extreme forms of demonstrating in favor of the standard political goal of eliminating discrimination toward a particular group, or an extreme form of the otherwise legitimate political opposition to it.

Americans are appalled by the divisiveness of the 2016 political season. But the 2012 season was divisive, too, and for largely the same reasons and over the same issues: Obamacare, immigration, inequality, race. The question is why. Why is divisiveness so pervasive in America today? The answer is that divisiveness is inevitable when property redistribution is in play, as it increasingly has been ever since group versus group politics began to replace the property rights of individuals, which has been happening in the United States for more than a century. Now all the Western countries, including the United States, are fully redistributionist in character, which is bound to maximize divisiveness, anger and violence, because the only acceptable political and social stance in such an environment is for you to join your group in being mad at the other group. In a redistributive environment, a group is easily turned into a mob, one whose members must show their anger as much as possible at all times as a means of demonstrating how they are being unfairly treated. Thus once government takes on the role of allocating outcomes, the anger of groups is a given, bound to seethe and grow as mobs fight over their shares of wealth, power, respect, dignity, etc., and the pressure to join and fight over such things becomes irresistible, a virtual political and social necessity.

The change from individual rights to group rights and from capitalism to socialism began in the United States with the Civil War, which was not really about the freeing of slaves, as history would have it, but about the establishment of what was effectively a giant affirmative action program for blacks that is still with us, and is the source of all the anger on both sides, as well as for the lack of progress for blacks today. The Civil War was also the actual beginning of the policy known in recent decades with justified derision as "nation building," which has been an abject failure, costing trillions of dollars and thousands of American lives as it has harmed our security and led to the rise of thousands, perhaps millions of enemies, including al Qaeda and ISIS. I bring up these two policies together here to make the point that the two—affirmative action at home, aka redistribution, and nation building abroad—are basically the same policy implemented in different spheres. They are both based on the change from protecting the rights of individuals, such as property rights and the right to the pursuit of happiness, to an assumed need to see individual people as members of groups who are due "civil" rights so they can make "progress" against each other *as groups*.

Neither policy has ever worked, even if reduced to its lowest common denominator questions, such as: Has affirmative action helped blacks in America? Or: Has nation building made America safer? The answer to both questions is a resounding "No." If affirmative action has worked for blacks generally, as opposed to having helped a few lucky beneficiaries of it, then why do we still see growing numbers of Black Lives Matter demonstrations and riots in Chicago, Baltimore and dozens of other cities? And if nation building has worked, why has my prediction proved correct that "the number and strength of our enemies will expand without limit" in response? That prediction on the first page of this book was written just as President Bush was renaming the policy nine days after 9/11. He would now call it "the War on Terror," and quickly demanded and got the United Nations to require all of its 189 member states to join us in it, an effective expansion of nation building that has been another predictable and predicted disaster described in this book. [See the final chapter, Afterward, to learn why this jointly pursued policy of the United States and the United Nations makes Muslims hate us both.]

Nation building is the modern remnant of the "roving institutions of freedom" unleashed by the Emancipation Proclamation, which encouraged slaves to escape from their plantations and fight for freedom. Because the first draft of the Proclamation seemed to invite war crimes and atrocities by the escaping or escaped slaves—"servile rebellions"—it was revised to officially outlaw such atrocities *even though rebellion was still encouraged*, thus creating what became the modern rules of war, as suggested by historian John Fabian Witt [see pages 57-60 of *Nature's God*]. The relevant point here is that the South was a society that the United States thought it had the moral authority to change fundamentally by force, and it encouraged rebellion in that society by its discontents, the slaves. The policy presumes that we know how other societies should be run and have the right to encourage rebellions within them that our armies may assist them with in order to impose our preferred social order upon them. Modern manifestations of the policy, always with at least some effort to bring along the United Nations as a partner, include our encouragement of rebellions by suppressed majorities to overthrow dictators in Iraq, Syria and Libya, all of which have been spectacular failures, including Iraq, where a Shiite-run "inclusive democracy" designed by us is serving primarily as a training ground for ISIS and other terrorists who want to attack Americans and America. It was obvious that something like this would be the outcome of the policy since long before 9/11. In fact, the policy has always been practically and theoretically flawed, as well as morally suspect, ever since President Lincoln invented it a century and a half ago.

While nation building to transform a slave society in another nation to one that does not allow slavery may seem ethically sound, there are two problems with it that become clear upon reflection. First, now that we are asserting our right to forcibly transform other societies to those that are not steeped in real sins like slavery, as the South was, but are merely non-democratic or non-pluralistic, the moral claim has dissolved. So far, we haven't even figured out how to get Shiites, Sunnis and Kurds to stop killing each other in Iraq, for example, which was much more peaceful and even progressive under Saddam than it is now. And Syria, Libya, Afghanistan and many other nations we tried to help with our nation building are joining Iraq as failed states that are breeding grounds for the terrorism we meant to suppress, not to mention sources of unending floods of refugees. But just imagine how much worse it will get when we add in the more modern elements of our diversity rainbow, such as women's and LGBT rights. Muslim societies are at least as opposed to these as southern plantation owners were to freeing their slaves. So how exactly will transgender bathrooms in Baghdad make us safer at home?

Second, since slavery was eliminated in every other country but the United States without civil wars or emancipation proclamations inciting "servile rebellions" within them, it is not true that we would still have slavery today if we hadn't imposed those violent convulsions on our country. Whether through various schemes of "compensated emancipation" that had been floated; or through the practice of important countries like England declaring slaves free if they touched their soil, whether because they had escaped or had landed there or at one of the colonies in their empire during travels of the slave trade; or through the refusal of such countries to accommodate in their laws the demands of slaveholders to return their human "property;" or whether making use of the obvious opportunity of a country like the United States, whose laws were based on "certain unalienable rights," such as that to the pursuit of happiness, whose courts could have easily determined that such a right is incompatible with the ownership of one human being by another (yes, the Supreme Court could have actually done some good at one time!)— Slavery would have faded from the scene on its own. If the South had been allowed to secede, not only would it have moved past slave labor to free labor by itself, it would have been able to help keep up both the South and the North economically through trade, which it would have naturally done if only the century-long economic trauma imposed by the Civil War hadn't intervened. The South would have maintained many commercial connections with the North and eventually might have even reconnected politically to it once the South was no longer dependent economically on slave labor.

Whether or not all elements of this road-not-traveled would have happened, the one that matters for our purposes here certainly would have: slavery would have long since vanished, because America's slaves did not need the Civil War or the Emancipation Proclamation to free them. They would have been freed anyway at latest by some time in the twentieth century, as happened without war in all other slave-holding societies around the world, mostly in the nineteenth century. So those who claim that blacks and the South and the United States had to go through the whole race versus race nightmare to get to a world where African Americans were able to exercise their own right to the pursuit of happiness are mistaken. Further, and most important, because the first step on that tortured path, the Civil War, set the stage for the rest of it— Reconstruction, Black Codes, the KKK, lynch mobs, Jim Crow, desegregation, busing, white flight, re-segregation, Ferguson, Black Lives Matter, the Emanuel 9 massacre—not only would we have skipped the most tragic and violent war in history, we would not be on the path that led to Ferguson and Charleston today.

For all our good nation building and affirmative action intentions behind freeing the slaves, there has been nothing but black versus white conflict ever since, and it is still getting worse even after 156 years of trying. The reason is that the policy itself, at any level of success at improving the lot of blacks relative to whites, is bound to perpetuate and exacerbate conflict and anger, as any redistributive policy must. While universal pre-K or reparations payments to blacks for the nation's sin of slavery, as some have advocated, would help some blacks relative to whites, the problem of black versus white conflict would only increase under such policies for the simple reason that, once redistribution is initiated, there will never come a time when those on the receiving end or their political advocates will say they have had enough. In both affirmative action and nation building, the assumption is that votes, the ballot box, is the proper way to allocate outcomes in society, offsetting differences in wealth, incomes, dignity and other measures via such means as redistributive taxes and redistributive programs in health, education and housing. Such policies will never lead to the social harmony their advocates predict, but will instead always lead to discord and anger at best, and ultimately to riots, violence, civil war, ethnic cleansing and genocide.

Perhaps the best example is the creation of the newest nation in the world, South Sudan (number 193), by the United States, the United Nations and others in July 2011, which sprang almost instantly into ethnic cleansing and genocide as the government of "national unity" sponsored by its well-intentioned wishful thinkers in the international community fell apart. The problem was the inability of the two main ethnic groups to trust democracy in their forced mixing, which caused instant atrocities that have never let up:

> South Sudan Forms New Coalition Government of National Unity. South Sudan's leaders have formed a transitional coalition government bringing together politicians from the government and the armed opposition who have been at war for two and a half years. The new government is led by President Salva Kiir and former rebel leader Riek Machar, who returned to the capital Juba on Tuesday to take up the post of vice president. Kiir named 16 of

the new government's 30 Cabinet ministers while Machar nominated 10. Four others were selected by political groups outside Kiir and Machar's factions. The government, which has a 30-month mandate culminating in fresh elections, has been formed according to a peace deal signed by Kiir and Machar last August under intense pressure from the international community. Tens of thousands were killed in South Sudan's civil war since 2013 after a falling out between Kiir and Machar. [Jason Patinkin, Associated Press, Juba, South Sudan—April 29, 2016]

This latest US/UN-sponsored attempt at national unity in 2016 is virtually identical to the first one they sponsored at the launch of the new democracy in 2011. But because Kiir is a Dinka, the largest ethnic group (which got him the presidency), and Machar is a Nuer, the second largest ethnic group (which got him the vice presidency), both of their ethnic groups realized immediately that they were in a cage match sponsored by the United States and the United Nations and that defending themselves against the other group required aggressive violence, the sooner the better. The goal was to kill or ethnically cleanse your rivals before they could do the same to you on the way to voting your property and political power away. Five years on and numerous new attempts at a "government of national unity" later, three hundred thousand people have been killed, over a million have been displaced internally, and four hundred thousand have fled to neighboring countries.

The one thing certain is that this latest one won't work either, any more than similar nation building arrangements the US has tried in Iraq, Afghanistan, Libya, Syria, Bosnia, Kosovo, Serbia, Somalia, Palestine and many other "peace processes" and "Dayton Accords" around the world. In all of them, the fundamental problem is that these agreements treat people as groups, defined mostly in ethnic, religious, or national origin terms, such as Shiites, Sunnis and Kurds (or Dinkas and Nuers, or Tutsis and Hutus, or Jews and Palestinians), sometimes spiced up recently by pressure to include women and LGBT categories, too. The assumption is that, with the help of our advice on how to fairly share among the groups in the organization of the government, and with the muscle provided by our coalition-of-the-willing soldiers and "blue helmets" from the UN, they can work toward a proper democracy that might someday function as ours does in, say, Dayton, Ohio.

None of this will ever work, because it can't work. In fact, it doesn't even work in Dayton anymore, or Chicago or Baltimore or St.

Louis (Ferguson), to pick just a few of the recent Black Lives Matter flashpoints. If government sets itself up to redress unfair distribution, whatever its origins—including from grossly inhuman atrocities or war crimes—as measured by group versus group calculations of fairness or justice, both or all affected parties will be perpetually mad at the opposing group and at government, regardless of the measurements, and regardless of the logic of the claims or their illogic, and regardless of whether adjustments have been made in the past to address them, or are expected to be made in the future.

Take equal pay for equal work, a favorite of women's groups, which often claim that women in the United States make only 78% of what men make for the same work, a claim that regularly underlies political calls for various kinds of new laws and rules in the workplace that will provide special help for women to offset the presumed discrimination and unfairness imposed by men. But the concept of "equal work" is ridiculous. It implies that a particular job is so fixed and rigid in what it is and requires that everyone who does it could and should always be paid the same. This is not true of any job, much less of all jobs. To take an obvious example, a 25-year-old man, a 45-year-old man and a 65-year-old man should all be paid the same, according to the equal pay logic, regardless of the differences that either the employee or the employer might recognize between them, such as experience, maturity, family status, future time and prospects with the company, training at the job, competence at the job, time to retirement, etc., all of which could easily affect performance for that employee at any particular job. And age is just one of hundreds or thousands of such factors that would make it impossible to determine what "equal work" is. The same would be true for women, both considered against each other and against the men, and even before taking account of such obvious differences as their potentially different interest in having and raising children.

Further, regardless of whether new policies are adopted to address the supposed problem of unequal pay, the arguments will continue no matter how the measurements change or how much "progress" is made. If women's pay reached 88% of men's pay, or 98% or 108% or 208%—the arguments would continue, as they have even after women and girls began to substantially exceed the performance and participation of men in terms of educational achievement in both high school and college, a result that may at least partly have come from the special help given them via Title IX and other means of leveling the playing field. The same kinds of calculations also are brought in from other than pay metrics, such as the percentage of women in management, the C-suite, on corporate boards, in venture capital, in technology, or in STEM fields. According to this line of thinking, anything less than the presumed fair result of 50% is unacceptable, since women are about 50% of the population.

Similarly, anything less than the percentage of African Americans or other minorities at any of these levels is considered unacceptable if it is less than the percentage of them in the relevant populations. Because the arguments will continue as a political strategic imperative at any level of "success" or "progress" at addressing the inequities or, for that matter, failure to do so, the anger will remain and grow. As long as government is perceived to be in charge of the distribution of fairness, wealth, dignity, etc., viewing people as members of groups will always lead to disappointment, because the assumption will be that the government could have done better for your group. Such disappointment is bound to lead to demonstrations or worse as a sense of permanent grievance at any level of income, wealth or acceptance of the members of any of these groups by the society at large drives them all to push for a better deal by visibly expressing their anger.

So it is not the lingering discrimination that is holding blacks back; it is the attempt to extinguish discrimination that is holding them back. If you are black and believe that whites are always stopping your progress either because of their racism or because of their unwillingness to grant sufficient diversity, inclusion or "safe spaces," much less universal pre-K or reparations, as some advocate, then you will always be mad. And if you are white and see your group held back by the presumed need to give special advantages to blacks to offset discrimination, you'll be mad, too. People who are perpetually mad at each other—and getting madder all the time as the political imperative of a redistributive environment—will never be able to work well together or be integrated into normal society. So blacks and whites get further and further apart as a direct result of the official attempts by government to bring them together.

Even seeming successes under these conditions suffer from a disingenuousness that stems from their forced integration—a phony friendship here, a cooperative business alliance there—but with no real feeling or joy, as if you were just ticking a diversity box to impress friends, bosses, or whoever is looking, something to see on your Facebook wall, list in your resume, mention in your college application essay.

Although satisfying and genuine relationships no doubt break through the pretense from time to time, they too must be tainted by a need on both sides of an interracial relationship to be wary, to wonder if you are giving enough recognition to the bigger picture, the racial picture, as it affects or afflicts one or both of your hopes and dreams, not to mention each of your expectations of proper behavior by the other person in light of those hopes and dreams in an environment dominated by government-policy-based redistribution. Studies show, such as in Claude Steele's *Whistling Vivaldi*, that both whites and blacks underperform in mixed social situations if they are afraid of appearing to be insensitive or unable to effectively navigate the appropriate behavior in such situations, and especially when there is a "stereotype threat" experienced by one or both people, which there is bound to be when the ideal behavior is practically unattainable by either party.

Most people are aware of how performance anxiety can cause you to choke and underperform because of the very fear that you will do just that, such as because of excess nervousness when giving a speech to a large audience or when trying to act appropriately at a party. Stereotype threat is a particular kind of such performance anxiety leading to choking that results from your awareness that your group stereotypically underperforms at a given task or in a given field, or at least is viewed by you and others as likely to do so. If you are aware of the stereotype and so are others, and all eyes are watching you, the pressure can make it even more likely that you will stereotypically fail, as numerous experiments described in *Whistling Vivaldi* demonstrate. Blacks may fear they will do poorly on tests requiring intellectual ability—the stereotype—and can be made by an experimenter to do even worse on such tests if they are made more aware of this reputation, or stereotype, before or during the test, because such awareness makes them extra nervous and thus less able to perform than they would be otherwise. Similarly, women may do worse on math or science tests if they are made more aware by the experimenter that women have a reputation of doing poorly on such tests. In other words, they choke if they are made aware of the stereotype, but may do just fine on the same test if not made aware of the stereotype, or negative expectation that they and others have of them.

Such experiments as those described by Steele have demonstrated that stereotype threat is a real phenomenon and have generated hopes that relations between the races and sexes may be improved by figuring out how to mitigate it, such as by having everyone become aware through reading and instruction about dangers like stereotype threat so they can help each other find "safe spaces" where those dangers are reduced. If that could be done, not only might it reduce racial and other tensions, it might also give those that suffer from stereotype threat a way to do better in school or perhaps enable them to enter and excel in careers they previously assumed they were not cut out for. Those who suffer from discrimination—women, blacks, transgenders—are understandably interested in seeing whether new policy based on such research could improve their lot. Unfortunately, it won't be that easy.

In a curious twist on stereotype threat, whites often fear they have among blacks a reputation for being racists, or closet racists, or are at least racially insensitive, a view that could easily convince whites they may perform poorly in mixed race situations where both blacks and whites will be watching their performance. Hence, whites have a stereotype threat problem that may cause them to perform even more poorly or awkwardly in mixed race situations precisely because of their reputation, even if they are not racist or insensitive in any measurable way. But it is indeed a stereotype threat problem because it can be exaggerated if a white man is made aware by an experimenter of his group's reputation for being insensitive just as his sensitivity is being tested. In other words, whites' desire to be sensitive, to not make a racial sensitivity mistake, is a new category of social performance to be anxious about and thus fail at precisely because of that anxiety. In the worst case (fear of which will *really* make him nervous), a white man might appear to be guilty of "unconscious bias" or a "micro-aggression" as he chokes and says just the wrong thing at precisely the wrong time in his attempts to be sensitive.

A white person may have read or heard, for example, that blacks are offended at being called "articulate" as a compliment, as this indicates that the white person has not heard that blacks feel condescended to and disrespected when this word is used with respect to them, as if they are not expected to be articulate. Now, even if the white person is aware of this history and would thus avoid the "articulate" word when speaking of black people, he may worry and be nervous that there are other words that he might unknowingly use that would offend, and in particular that he might be perceived as having used them knowingly or deliberately, in which case he would be guilty of a "micro-aggression." Since, prior to having heard that calling blacks "articulate" could offend them, he would not have suspected that such a compliment would be offensive, he might understandably worry—and have performance anxiety about—the possibility that he could be tripped up by many other hidden dangers when attempting to talk with or about black people.

Thus whites may fear that, no matter how they try to keep up with the changing protocols of interracial conversation and relations, they will always be behind on the latest issues, concepts and charged words and therefore experience an ever-escalating and unsolvable stereotype threat problem that will cause them to choke and appear to be insensitive to blacks precisely because of their earnest attempts to become sensitive combined with their understandable and realistic fear that they will fail at it. Whites are not blacks, after all. So how could they possibly keep up with the true views and sensitivities of blacks, as expressed and felt by blacks among themselves, no matter how hard they try? And if they can't, there will always be a stereotype threat problem. In fact, even if a few very adept whites did manage to successfully navigate the social minefield, there would be no way for the bulk of them to escape the stereotype threat problem any more than the bulk of tennis players could escape their natural fear of failure and consequent tendency to choke if forced to play on centre court at Wimbledon. In fact, why wouldn't the field of racial sensitivity competition be just as unforgiving and as likely to support only a few winners and many also-rans as any other field of competition? And if it would, how could the attempt to corral stereotype threat or extinguish it ever be successful?

And never mind whites: If blacks, women, transgenders and everyone else of all races and ethnicities and sexes and sexual preferences wanting to be sensitive in the new and unfamiliar competition to mitigate stereotype threat suddenly realized that some people in their group were always going to be better than others at this competition—in fact that there would always be only a few winners and that most people would therefore be losers who are expected to underperform—wouldn't they all have a perpetual stereotype threat problem, just as whites do with blacks? Just as whites are not blacks, men are not women, and heterosexuals are not Ls, Gs, Bs or Ts, the impossibility of anyone's being as knowledgeable about the sensitivities of a group he is not in will lead to a perpetual problem where everyone will expect that someone not of a group will probably not be as sensitive as he could be if he were perfect, or were a star player in the competition to not give offense. Therefore, since only a few people can be stars, the bulk of people of any description will always have a stereotype threat problem no matter how hard they and others try to mitigate it, such as by reading and following the advice in *Whistling Vivaldi*. If the only way to get past this problem is if somehow everyone could be assumed by everyone else to be able to perform like a star player at all times in the sensitivity competition, and this is practically speaking impossible, how could this whole exercise to mitigate stereotype threat and create safe spaces ever be successful? In fact, by highlighting the fact that you are in this competition in which most people like you are poor players and likely to fail, wouldn't the effort to reduce stereotype threat itself cause the problem it is meant to address, just as reminding a woman that women aren't good at math right in the middle of a math test would?

In any case, Steele's book has become a virtual handbook on some college campuses, required reading for all incoming freshmen at Princeton, for example, its precepts spreading to many other universities that are emulating Princeton's orientation program run by its former Outing Club (now called Outdoor Action), with new students advised to discuss *Whistling Vivaldi* around the campfire to learn how to make safe spaces available to minorities so that their educational experience will be successful and therefore Princeton's goal of increasing diversity and inclusion will be maximized. It is hard to imagine a program more devoted to doing what the best minds, such as Steele, recommend to make sure that everyone is comfortably and productively included.

And yet even Princeton has seen large and disruptive demonstrations by Black Lives Matter through an affiliate called the Black Justice League that took over (occupied) the President's office to demand that former Princeton President and United States President Woodrow Wilson's name be removed from the Woodrow Wilson School of Public and International Affairs, and from Wilson College, a residential college, and that other evidence of his history at Princeton be erased because, according to the protesters, he was a racist. Illustrating that anger will only increase in this redistributive environment as long as groups are measured against each other in terms of their "progress," the Princeton community, its trustees, its president, its faculty, students and alumni made heroic efforts to reach a reasoned judgment on what to do about the Woodrow Wilson legacy. The special task force on Wilson's legacy added to a pre-existing year-old task force on diversity policy, concluding with a "call for a renewed and expanded commitment to diversity and inclusion," which soon resulted in the hiring of Princeton's first Dean for Diversity and Inclusion. This accommodation did not satisfy the Black Justice League, however, since the task forces did not recommend removing Wilson's name from any of Princeton's schools or colleges even though they acknowledged that his views on race would not have been acceptable today, a century after he was at Princeton.

For reference, Princeton has gone in the half century since I graduated from being almost all white and male to being significantly more diverse now. According to the task force report:

> Fifty years later there is evidence of progress. The undergraduate student body this year includes 48% women; 11.8% international students; and 42.5% American minorities (7.6% African American, 0.1 American Indian, 21.5% Asian American, 9.2% Latino/Hispanic, 4.0% multiracial non-Hispanic, and 0.2% Pacific Islander). Princeton has a thriving LGBT center and a highly regarded Center for Jewish Life.

While this may sound impressive, the likelihood that it will be perceived as inadequate by the forces of diversity and inclusion is evident in various quotes from the Alumni Weekly:

> A year after a University task force offered an ambitious set of proposals to make the campus more inclusive, Princeton officials say substantial progress has been made *but that much remains to be done.* [My emphasis here and below]

Such sentiments echo those of the new Dean of Diversity and Inclusion, who starts in August 2016, and also those of the vice provost for institutional equity and diversity, who said:

> We are making good progress, *but we still have a lot of work to do.*

Such comments are de rigueur, a mandatory mantra of diversity and inclusion advocates, to be found in any given speech by President Obama or any of his appointed agency or department heads speaking on almost any topic. Whether noting how far blacks have come since Brown or the Civil Rights Act, or how far women have come since Title IX, or how far gays have come since Stonewall, everyone celebrates the latest milestones—gay marriage, transgender bathrooms, women's soccer and graduation rates, etc.—while in the next breath issuing a call to arms in the form of the obligatory *"we still have a lot of work to do."* As President Obama tweeted on March 8, 2016:

We've come a long way on women's equality, *but there's still so much work to be done.*

Or when he tweeted on March 11, 2013 about the economy, which was (and still is) failing the middle class:

Our economy has come a long way over the last four years—*and we have more work to do.*

Or when Labor Secretary Thomas Perez tells a Future of Work Symposium in Washington, D.C. in December 2015:

We passed the Equal Pay Act, *though we've certainly got some unfinished business to close the gap between women's earnings and men's.*

Or his remarks to the National Action Network 25th Anniversary, April 13, 2016:

Undeniable progress and *pressing unfinished business*—those are really the two fundamental truths of America as we sit here today.

What all this shows is that politicians and leaders across our society see groups and their claims against each other first, and then build political platforms and factions around those groups' righteous anger over their still downtrodden status and unfair treatment. These leaders invariably think all those groups will be happier if the leaders have a free hand at manipulating outcomes. But they won't, because at best there will be only "progress" or a compromise leaving all the tensions broiling— *and much more work to be done.* What is really astonishing is how these leaders support this anger- and violence-inducing view while actually believing they are reducing tensions with it. From The Boss bothered by bigotry to House Speaker Paul Ryan or Apple CEO Tim Cook or any number of other politicians or CEOs saying "that's not who we are" about such things as immigration restrictions or religious freedom laws, all leaders feel immune to criticism if they support a policy of banning discrimination, apparently ignorant entirely of both its potential to *cause* anger, rather than reduce it, and of the fact that no such policies existed at the founding of America.

But we are on a treadmill now, one we can't get off. When everyone involved in the academic enterprise devotes large amounts of their time to imbibing and administering diversity and inclusion propaganda, and the main result is still anger, it is clear that more than time has been lost. When the one and only irreducible goal of the exercise to accommodate Black Lives Matter or incorporate *Whistling Vivaldi* into diversity and inclusion policy is to reduce anger, and the result is still anger *(because more needs to be done)* in spite of everyone's best efforts, the authors of the policies should reassess their basic premises. When all institutions of higher learning are constantly beset with arguments over "trigger warnings," "micro-aggressions" and other supposed evidence that they are not taking discrimination seriously, but the more they try to sincerely address the complaints the madder everyone gets *(because more needs to be done),* it is reasonable to conclude there is something wrong with their approach.

The university, of course, is not the only modern institution overwhelmed by its "responsibility" to spread diversity and inclusion propaganda and the associated requirement to change core policies and practices in fundamental ways. All large corporations and government entities, including the police and the military, are also required to spend large amounts of their time and energy becoming showcases for diversity and inclusion. As a result, while these policies will perpetually disappoint in terms of reducing tensions, they will also cause the organizations that adopt them to be increasingly ineffective at their previous tasks, such as making profits or protecting people from crime or terrorists. To pick an obvious example everyone is familiar with: How can an airport security system obsessing over the profiling sensitivities of those it screens ever protect us, or even get us through the lines and onto the planes?

The main purpose of this chapter is to call attention to this fact: Rather than reducing tension and violence in our society, the universally embraced goal of eliminating discrimination is actually the primary cause of that tension and that violence, inciting both domestically inspired riots and their "senseless act" offshoots, as well as an increasing risk that the escalations of terrorism caused by our War on Terror will at some point bump into the reality that nukes and other WMD will inevitably be deployed during those escalations.

President Obama likes to pretend that his version of the war is different from that of the Bushes and other Republicans. But it's not. He calls it something different, but has actually expanded it more than anyone, with American forces operating in 7 countries officially and up to 150 countries if measured by the hidden war of drones and "special" forces. Moreover, he has done more than anyone to justify it in terms that are specifically related to America's anti-discrimination jihad, such as when he told a mostly Muslim Cairo audience in 2009:

> I consider it part of my responsibility as President of the United States to fight against negative stereotypes of Islam wherever they appear.

But like all the other presidents, whether their versions of the war were styled as protecting borders, protecting people from starvation, protecting people from dictators, or protecting *our* oil or the "new world order," President Obama has expanded it drastically:

> The presidency of Barack Obama coincided with the "golden age" of America's special operations, according to General Joseph Votel, who in 2014 assumed the reins of U.S. Special Operations Command (SOCOM). In the decades since the embarrassing Iran hostage rescue mission—subsequently enshrined as "our most successful failure"—the special operations community had grown and prospered. With over seventy-two thousand personnel and further expansion projected, SOCOM by 2015 was on track to surpass the entire British Army in overall size. Over the course of the previous year, SOCOM had operated in an astonishing 150 countries. No military force in history had acquired such a far-flung presence. [*America's War for the Greater Middle East: a military history*, Andrew J. Bacevich, Random House, 2016, Kindle location 6076]

In spite of President Obama's significant expansion of the war, not only has it harmed the stability and security of all of the foreign countries it was designed to help (as it did during his predecessors' administrations), it has failed even more miserably at its principle mission of making Americans safer in their own country (as did his predecessors' versions of the war).

To bring home how dangerous these twin instigators of violence could be—the anti-discrimination jihad at home and nation building abroad—just imagine how their accidental or deliberate merger might unfold. People have forgotten that Oklahoma City bomber Timothy McVeigh had a probable Middle-Eastern connection, a theory that was dropped like a hot potato almost as soon as it was suggested:

On the contrary, the Clinton administration adopted the party line that the bombing was planned and executed by two white male types. The president himself predictably attacked "two right-wing fanatics" and indicted conservative talk show hosts for their incendiary language calculated to incite the Timothy McVeighs of the nation to launch such attacks. [*The Third Terrorist: the Middle East Connection to the Oklahoma City Bombing*, Jayna Davis, 2004, Nelson Current, Foreword by David P. Schippers, Fmr. Chief Investigative Counsel for the impeachment trial of President Bill Clinton, Kindle location 52]

Ignoring that connection apparently fit in more comfortably with our preferred political narratives, just as the Benghazi attack that killed an ambassador and three other Americans was supposedly the result of an anti-Muslim video made by a domestic right wing nut from Oregon, or that 9/11 was supposedly the result of Muslims who hated freedom, or that Saddam Hussein supposedly had WMD, all of which were narratives designed accidentally or deliberately to buttress a dominant political party and president in America looking to expand his version of the War on Terror. So instead of calling McVeigh a Muslim terrorist, he was just considered to be a bigger version of what Dylann Roof is the latest example of, i.e., an antigovernment redneck and racist, and the potential Middle Eastern connection was ignored.

But if McVeigh's senseless act was actually an example of how our preferred political narratives were keeping us from connecting the dots to foreign terrorism, which was eventually acknowledged to be why 9/11 snuck up on us; if Benghazi was not about a spontaneous reaction of street crowds to a video but about serious Muslim terrorists attacking us because of our War on Terror; if the Muslims who attacked us on 9/11 didn't do it because they hated freedom but because they hated us intervening in their world with what used to be called nation building but is now called the War on Terror; if the story of how Saddam Hussein had WMD was just blatant bull to justify invading Iraq—if all of these stories were nothing but convenient narratives designed to enable us to keep the politics in play that would enable our various presidents to wage our unending war by drawing attention away from its main consequence: the creation of terrorism, then imagine what else we are missing: How many ISIS or al Qaeda sleepers are sneaking in with immigrants from Mexico or under "fiancé visas" from Syria or other Muslim countries, as one of the San Bernardino murderers did? How many Black Lives Matter sympathizers or Imaaiyl Brinsleys are also sympathetic with or supported by ISIS, al Qaeda, Boko Haram, Al-Shabaab or the Taliban? How many African Americans have changed their names to Muslim names in solidarity with "Black Muslims" or other Black Power movements like Black Lives Matter, which apparently inspired even black women graduates of West Point in 2016 to raise their fists in solidarity in a controversial and unauthorized group photo? How many of these black women and men are sympathetic with the radical redistribution goals and the disruptive and violent demonstration methods that Black Lives Matter routinely uses and encourages others to adopt in order to achieve those goals? Even if only one percent of African Americans agree with such goals and methods, and even if only one percent of *them* would link their own oppression to the also discriminated against Muslims, as President Obama did in his 2009 Cairo speech, the results could be devastating. In a WMD age, and with a little help from their friends, it would only take one Timothy McVeigh, one Dylann Roof or one Ismaaiyl Brinsley— "Watch what I'm going do," "Reparations Matter!" "Allahu Akbar"—to kill dozens, hundreds, thousands or millions.

Given the risks posed by our antidiscrimination jihad—the dominant political narrative in America today and the one that underlies all of our interventions at home and abroad—it is worth a serious attempt to reassess whether eliminating discrimination is now or ever has been a good idea. Since the belief that it is a good idea is deeply embedded, I will suggest in the final pages of this chapter three unusual approaches to breaking the mental logjam that is preventing the reassessment I am recommending. First, we'll consider how permitting discrimination could actually reduce tension, rather than increase it, as conventional wisdom would expect. Second, we'll look again at Harper Lee's famous book, *To Kill A Mockingbird*, as we reconsider what it says. And finally, we'll have another look at The Gettysburg Address.

Rethinking Discrimination

As I describe in all my books but most completely in *Nature's God*, trying to eliminate discrimination runs counter to network formation because it disrupts its driving force, what network scientists call "preferential attachment" or "rich get richer." This force, which is practically speaking synonymous with "discrimination," drives the creation of all the harmonious arrangements in human society, from ethical institutions such as religions and those of marriage and family, to the business monopolies that made America a wealthy and powerful nation, all of which are networks. Like species settling into their niches in an ecosystem as the fit ones rise and the unfit disappear, the competition among networks whose formation is driven by preferential attachment results in cooperative and accommodative arrangements where all the "creatures" are, literally, dependent on each other and therefore tend to get along. That is, they naturally adjust to each other's presence in a way that takes account of their different strengths and weaknesses, using each other "parasitically" whenever possible (i.e., in the good ecological sense of the term, which describes how everything in an ecosystem is related to and dependent on everything else), even though at any given time some are rising in importance and others are receding or going extinct.

The key thing about preferential attachment is that it must be allowed to operate freely, which is to say without coercion by government, a freedom I have likened to "the pursuit of Happiness" and "the Laws of Nature and of Nature's God" in our Declaration of Independence. Not that the Founders were familiar with network science, which would not be popular for a couple centuries. But with these ringing phrases they were clearly trying to create a society where people were free to choose their associates—personal, social or business—and for nearly a century, they were.

Our society is falling apart today, disintegrating into rancor, anger and violence, because harmony has been disrupted by the attempt to ban discrimination, and has thereby turned the organization of society into what is effectively a government program to rebalance the races, ages, sexes, gender preferences, income and wealth groupings, etc. One way to think of this government program and understand why it is harmful is to recognize that it is just another instance of the eugenics mania that seized many Western countries in the early- to mid-twentieth century, including America, which conducted forced sterilizations of 70,000 "imbeciles," and Nazi Germany, which mainly tried to exterminate all Jews, but went after Gypsies, cripples and other "undesirables" like "imbeciles," too. With eugenics again effectively driving American policy as politicians reorder the relations between groups according to the latest greatest theories, it is no wonder we're going off the rails, with large majorities of Americans regularly telling pollsters we are on the wrong track. Today's government is not only denying the people their right to choose their associates freely, which makes them mad to begin with, it is doing so under the mistaken belief that government can itself do all the deciding for us about how things should fit together, right down to such details as who must be allowed in our bathrooms. So we have more and more senseless acts as government makes everyone mad in general and makes some people mad enough to kill.

Perhaps now would be a good time to rethink a few of our assumptions about discrimination. First, just because someone has the right to discriminate negatively against someone by choosing to not associate with him does not mean that he will do so. In fact, the opposite is more likely the case: if he is *free* to discriminate, he is *less likely* to discriminate. If a person is free to associate or not with another person, it is more likely that if he chooses to associate, whether for love, friendship or business, it will be a genuine connection that both parties are happy with. This prospect of a genuinely happy association, which is really only possible if both parties were truly free to make that connection or not, i.e., if they were not forced to make it by antidiscrimination laws, will likely lead to more cross-group relations rather than fewer, even if—and perhaps especially if—the parties would have been otherwise inclined against each other because of bigotry or racism. In contrast, if a person is forced to make a connection that he does not want to make, both parties will have reason to doubt if the connection is sincere or genuinely in either of their interests. At the extreme, mandated connections will be unhappy ones that can lead to social turmoil and violence. So the general rule is that if connections are freely chosen, they will be happy ones, while if potential connections are either not proposed or freely declined, they would not exist and thus would also be unlikely to cause tension or anger or violence. Thus the freedom to discriminate will be likely to lead to more association across groups, i.e., to less actual discrimination, than a ban on discrimination does.

But problems arise when a declined person or one that is not included in a group is told by his government that he had a civil right to be accepted by the people who declined or didn't include him, in which case he may think he has a right to their property, and may engage in violence against those people or their property—or, perhaps even worse, he may just feel lousy or even suicidal about his own place in society. Think about this the next time you see demonstrations turn into riots or hear about an atrocity committed against a black man by whites or against a white man by blacks, or against a gay person by heterosexuals. How much of that could have been avoided if people were free to make or decline to make normal connections in the ordinary course of their lives without government telling them what to do? How many atrocities could be avoided if people and businesses were free to not rent to, hire, serve, or use restrooms with those they would not have chosen on their own to rent to, hire, serve or use restrooms with?

How many atrocities against transgenders or transgender suicides could be avoided if transgenders were not given the impression by government that *all* of society had to accept them everywhere they want to go, including in what were once strictly private domains? Bathrooms, or showers or locker rooms, where people are routinely undressed, are inherently private spaces even if they are in "public accommodation" facilities, such as schools or parks or corporations or restaurants. So by setting the bar at *all*, when significant portions of society are not yet ready to accept transgenders as normal, the government has effectively maximized the likelihood that transgenders will be made to feel unwelcome or odd and has thereby maximized the likelihood of suicide or bullying or atrocities. Put another way, if people were not required to associate with or accept transgenders, but merely did so if they wanted to, the chances of rejection would be reduced, thus reducing both the astronomical suicide rate among transgenders and the likelihood that they will be bullied or subjected to violence.

That a supposedly compassionate society would subject individuals in the most vulnerable group to an identity acceptance test that, by design of "Justice" Department rules, requires 100% tolerance of that group, when it is almost certainly less than 1% of the population (probably only 0.2% or 0.3%) and still viewed as bizarre by most people, is an irony of soaring hypocrisy. And it will get worse, also by design.

Transgenders are by definition "transitioning," trying to figure out what they were "born" as, an entirely subjective determination which may or may not contain some element of their visible sex at birth. And in that process there is no endpoint. So whatever the most *unacceptable* choice is at any given moment, as determined in the mind of the most creative transgender among them, will tend to become the new most aggrieved and protected group, just as transgenders in general are now, who have for the moment stolen the grievance show from the better known and more numerous Ls, Gs and Bs. But once we know what this so far unnamed and unknown identity is, it will become for a while the group that the leading pundits of diversity demand acceptance of as their acceptance or non-rejection becomes the new litmus test of "who we are as a nation," just as is happening for transgenders now. And then this new group will be the aggrieved group du jour until another even more unacceptable and tinier minority identity shows up as a result of the perpetual transitioning experimentation. So, to summarize where we have come as a nation, we have gone from a time when we had to accept and provide special help for a well known group with an unquestioned pedigree of grievance based on hundreds of years of slavery, the identity of which was a question of black and white, to a situation where the Most Protected Group award is given to a constantly shape-shifting identity whose proliferating sexualities are competing for and aspiring to most-aggrieved status by aiming to become the *tiniest* minority possible, the one whose characteristics are *most unacceptable* to the *maximum number of people*.

And all this is happening even though it is still unclear if any of our special "protections" have ever even helped the black people they were originally designed for. How many poor black families, for example, were squeezed out of homes they couldn't afford when bankers were forced to give them mortgages they wouldn't have chosen to give them on their own? Redlining has a reputation of being an evil practice, but the truth is it is just good business to make such bulk judgments regarding the relative attractiveness of loaning money in one neighborhood versus another, and a lot of the poor black families that were hurt in the sub-prime crisis would not have been caught in it if bankers had not been forced by anti-redlining laws to give them loans.

Bulk judgments, or "shunning," are also common in the realms of morals and ethics, such as when religions proscribe having illegitimate children or homosexuality, and guide their adherents to shun people who engage in them. While societies at large are not smart enough through our proverbial "national conversations" to decide on and promote the good practices and suppress the bad ones, as long as people are free to choose their associates and religions, the mechanism of preferential attachment will sort through such issues naturally in a comfortable manner that will result in a happy society that is able to tolerate differences. Which is where network formation comes in. Most religions traditionally ban incest and many ban polygamy (although both Mormons and Muslims have mixed records on that score), just as, as mentioned above, almost all of them used to ban homosexuality and illegitimate children. Over time, human societies sort their preferences and moral positions out through their living and social and religious arrangements, which are the culminations of millions of individual decisions to accept or not accept (or, collectively, to shun) attachments, in the end comfortably settling in to what works for them.

But if government butts in and wrecks the process, all bets are off. Take the bans on illegitimate children and homosexuality, both of which appear to be on their last legs in America. Although it is by no means clear why, it is a fair bet that government policies that favor sexual diversity and working women played a role. Whatever the cause, soaring rates of illegitimacy and gay weddings make it ever harder to apply the old bans even if discrimination were still allowed in these matters, which it largely isn't. This effectively means that those old bans on illegitimate children and homosexuality are no longer allowed and therefore everyone—100% of us—must accept these practices no matter what religion we belong to or ethical views we have. This all leads to turmoil and conflict, especially since, at the same time, also floating around for acceptance, there are those mostly still banned practices of incest and polygamy vying for our moral allegiance. No wonder we're confused and angry.

I can't think of any of these practices that would not be as entitled to "equal dignity" as homosexuals are in the Supreme Court's 2015 decision on gay marriage. Aren't brothers and sisters, fathers and daughters, mothers and sons also entitled to equal dignity should they decide to marry? And why can't men "marry" multiple women, or women "marry" multiple men? In all of these situations, wouldn't everything from hospital visitation rights to inheritance laws to pension and health benefits be simplified if we let them "marry," just as the gay marriage advocates argued before the Supreme Court in 2015? Isn't this in fact required of state laws by the "equal protection" clause of the 14th Amendment and of federal laws by the "due process" clause of the 5th Amendment, as they argued then? These were the interpretations that snapped in place with those twin May 17, 1954 juggernaut decisions (Brown v. Board of Education and Bolling v. Sharpe) that teed up desegregation, initially haltingly but then forcefully ten years later via the Civil Rights Act of 1964 that outlawed discrimination based on race, color, religion, sex, or national origin. That Act led finally in 1966 to the Department of Health, Education and Welfare having the power to force Southern schools to meet mathematical racial quotas by busing in spite of promises by the Act's proponents in Congress that neither racial quotas nor busing would be required.

You could go crazy rummaging through this history because the reality is it's all part of the grand antidiscrimination hairball behind the Justice Department's mandate of transgender bathrooms in public schools. What it means is that now *every* kid—100% of them: black and white and every other kind of kid—has to figure out what "transgender" means, and must start doing so as soon as they start going to the bathroom at school, which will add a whole new dimension to what "universal pre-K" means. So just in order to force black and white kids to go to school together in the 1960s, the legal superstructure that gave us busing and desegregation has transmogrified into a requirement today to make really young children wonder if they were born with the right "gender" or should consider "transitioning." With all due respect to how we have been "perfecting our Union" since President Lincoln's Emancipation Proclamation got the giant affirmative action ball rolling, things have been getting progressively worse with every new ruling.

Sorting through such social organization issues is the historical and natural role of religions, neighborhoods, communities, corporations and other natural networks—including millions of minor ones, such as clubs of all kinds, sports leagues, fishing or hunting buddies, Tuesday bridge, Thursday bowling, Saturday barbecues, etc.—and if allowed to proceed normally, will result in a relatively harmonious and happy society. The choices we make, both as individuals and as social beings—to choose to attach to or to decline to attach to, to hire or not hire, to work for or not, to rent to or not, to serve or not, to join or not, to shun or not—these are the kinds of choices that will find the right mix of morals and practices for our society, but only if free from government involvement. If they involve coercion by government, they will instead create anger and dissatisfaction, and the social norms they come up with will be disruptive. Based on the fates of the religious liberty laws and bathroom bills, as well as the entire history of civil rights generally, our society has clearly lost the capacity to sort through such issues effectively and is therefore not anywhere close to being harmonious or happy. And everything we are doing to make it better is making it worse, much worse.

One more thing: Not only does the freedom to discriminate require not being coerced by government to make attachments that you would not make on your own, it also requires being allowed to make connections that government doesn't want you to make, like price fixing conspiracies. The monopolies in America, starting with the formation of the club-like New York Stock Exchange in the 1790s, depended on the freedom to discriminate at will in selecting their membership and structuring their exchange as they saw fit, including by price fixing. Although many of those membership and structure choices eventually became illegal under antitrust, before that happened they led to the great wealth of America, including what was as recently as 1975 a vast and prosperous middle class. Unfortunately, the Securities & Exchange

Commission (SEC) has viciously attacked the freedom to discriminate, particularly since 1975, when it opted instead for an anonymous electronic high-frequency trading market designed to take down the NYSE's monopoly (initially through its IPO "subsidiary," NASDAQ) by mandating multiple market competition on a "level playing field." As a result, the NYSE's and NASDAQ's market shares dropped from the high eighties to the low twenties under the SEC's punishments, which destroyed our capacity to create new companies and technologies, and thereby wiped out our accustomed high rates of growth in good jobs paying higher wages. This is why both productivity and the middle class are disappearing, and why—for the first time—kids in America can no longer expect to do better than their parents did.

Rethinking Mockingbird

If you felt betrayed that *To Kill A Mockingbird* hero Atticus Finch became a bigot in Harper Lee's second novel, *Go Set a Watchman*, try reading Mockingbird again. You will find that there is actually nothing in it that indicates Atticus would be a supporter of the forced integration of black and white communities or schools. Although he is indeed saintly as well as heroic in many respects, his moral compass had him view individuals as individuals, deserving of equal rights before the law, whether they were black or white or, for that matter, white trash. Granting full respect and rights before the law to individuals made Atticus willing at considerable personal peril to defend a black man wrongly accused of rape. But this did not mean that he would also, separately, advocate mixing the races in a manner that was coercive and bound to cause discord between them, and there is nothing in Mockingbird to imply that he would.

So why did millions of readers get the wrong impression? The answer apparently is that *To Kill a Mockingbird*, published in 1961, rolled across America during the civil rights era of the nineteen sixties when readers wanted to believe, as did the nation, that we might finally be able to expiate our sins of slavery, Reconstruction, the KKK and Jim Crow by desegregating schools and enacting other antidiscrimination and pro-integration measures that would lift blacks up as a group. So the national mood in favor of integration took over and made Atticus its hero. But the fact is that neither Atticus nor anyone else discussed any of these issues in Mockingbird, which is set in the Depression of the nineteen thirties, three decades before the civil rights sixties when it was released.

But the misinterpretation of Mockingbird is even more dramatic, because not only is there nothing in it to justify the misinterpretation, but Watchman—the original book from which Mockingbird emerged after three years of editing—did indeed discuss those integration issues, and the conflict between respecting individuals as individuals versus raising blacks up as a group creates the tension between Jean Louise (modeled after Harper Lee herself) and her father over what her father had meant by the moral lessons she received from him as a child.

Watchman presents the possibility that Atticus and others could be moral in terms of how they see and treat individuals, and at the same time wary of desegregation or other policies intended to help blacks as a group that would disrupt and bring dissension into both white and black communities and schools. All the key characters, and especially Jean Louise, (the grown up Scout—the child heroine and narrator of Mockingbird), struggle with or have opinions about the differences in these two approaches, often presented simply as racial prejudice and a willingness or not to contemplate change in such traditional Southern attitudes. Jean Louise is anguished as she compares the progressive attitudes in her adopted New York, which she accepts and believes in, to those in her old home town and, literally, throws up thinking her father misled her as a child into adopting these progressive, civil-rights-friendly views that she now holds as an adult, views that she sees he no longer holds and maybe never did, which would mean either that he misled her or that she misunderstood him. Either way, Jean Louise makes in Watchman the exact error that those millions of Mockingbird fans made when they turned Atticus into a civil rights hero, an error that is forcing most of them to indignantly reject Watchman now because it shows Atticus to be what they assumed he could not be: a bigot.

Watchman takes place in the 1950s as the Supreme Court issued rulings that began to set the races against each other as groups, such as Brown v. Board of Education in 1954. But both books were written just before—and Mockingbird was released at the height of—those tense and hopeful 1960s when it became anathema outside of the South to speak anything but positively of civil rights goals to improve the lives of blacks through desegregation. Readers saw the highly moral Atticus defending a black man in a bigoted town and simply assumed that, because *they* believed not only in respecting the individual rights of that black man, but also in elevating blacks as a group—and considered *themselves* moral for doing so—Atticus would have agreed with them. But they were wrong. Atticus was indeed the entirely moral hero they thought he was. But it would have been inconsistent with his individual-based moral view to assault the rights of those same individuals by forcing them to accommodate themselves to group-based social programs like desegregation or busing.

As a result of the Supreme Court's moves, not just Atticus, but also the almost as saintly black cook, Calpurnia (a stand-in mother for Scout when she was a child in the 1930s of Mockingbird), and many others in her black community, as well as whites like Atticus and Hank, Jean Louise's fiancé, were forced to deal with people in the 1950s of Watchman as members of black versus white racial groups where the blacks would or would not make "progress" against the whites. And so when a distraught Jean Louise asks her beloved Cal why she is treating her distantly with her "company manners," Calpurnia answers, "What are you all doing to us?" In other words, why are you whites standing in the way of black progress? While Jean Louise is relieved and comforted by Cal's confirmation that her love for her as a child was genuine, even this makes her more confused as to why or whether her father had misled her then.

In Mockingbird the best people were able, as Atticus and Calpurnia did, to see people as individuals. But doing so became much harder in Watchman, where blacks and whites pulled away from each other as they clustered and strategized with their own people on how to use or defend against—or have racist opinions about—the new environment and the people in it, and thus became adversaries. The main difference between the two books, dictated by the different times in which they were set, is not that Atticus is a different person—a bigot—but that government in the Watchman era had set the races against each other because of its aggressive race versus race policies. Those who think Atticus changed between books have just not read Mockingbird carefully. That is, they saw what they wanted to see, what would buttress their own moral view of themselves as civil rights champions, rather than what was actually in the book. Of course the list of those who thus misread Mockingbird probably includes the overwhelming majority of its 60 million fans.

One person that list would not include is Harper Lee herself, who wrote the original book, which was Watchman, to address those exact issues. She went hard on herself in the character modeled after her, Jean Louise, whose often clumsy struggle to reconcile the two views drives the plot of Watchman, vividly illustrating a dilemma that challenges her relationship with her father, her hometown and her country, and is not necessarily resolved even at the book's end. But it is hard to imagine that Lee herself was not aware as the decades went by and the accolades piled up that the country and the world had misread Mockingbird and the Academy Award-winning movie made from it starring Gregory Peck as Atticus. Lee must have known that Atticus was no more nor less a bigot in Watchman than he was in Mockingbird. Indeed, Jean Louise, too, is revealed to be a bigot in Watchman by Atticus's brother, Uncle Jack ("not a big one, just an ordinary turnip-sized bigot") as he endeavored to have her consider the possibility that her problems with her father may have had more to do with herself than with him. She was already aware of this possibility (it was why she threw up), but had great difficulty coming to grips with it, and was not necessarily resolved on what she should think about it even as the book ended.

The reality is that our country has embraced a means of reducing racial tension that is actually increasing it, a mass delusion that I see no evidence in either Mockingbird or Watchman that Harper Lee shared, thus making her uniquely positioned to hold a mirror up to America in the form of these books and say, "see?" While we may never know why she decided to publish Watchman in 2015, it is known that she had wanted to write a book "about race," and probably knew from our reaction to Mockingbird that our understanding of race was at best incomplete. She as much as anyone would have known that true social morality is far closer to the individual-based morality of Atticus presented in both Mockingbird and Watchman than the group-based version underlying civil rights that Mockingbird readers mistakenly thought Atticus advocated to Scout as a child, as did Jean Louise, who struggles with that seeming deception at least throughout most of Watchman.

Lee must have known these things because she wrote Watchman, the original book, to explain and illustrate these very issues. So two things must have been clear to her as she watched the disastrous and deteriorating state of modern race relations unfold. First, that Mockingbird alone had not been enough, because, whatever good it did for race relations, they were still going downhill in spite of it. Second, it was obvious that her readers were still confused about race, because they had adopted the same errors in thinking that Jean Louise had adopted, which tormented her throughout Watchman, errors which Lee wrote Watchman to illustrate. And so it surely would have occurred to Lee that allowing readers to see how Jean Louise dealt with those same errors and that same confusion in Watchman might help them understand what they had missed in Mockingbird. Although Lee would have known that releasing Watchman could harm her reputation—and it did, at least so far; many have said they will never read Mockingbird again, or Watchman, and some have revived discredited speculation that maybe the reclusive Lee didn't even really write Mockingbird, that maybe it was her editor's work or her old friend Truman Capote's, on whom the character of Dill was based—she might also have hoped it would help readers better understand race by correcting the errors that they and Jean Louise had embraced about what Atticus was telling Scout in Mockingbird. It was a risky and bold move, something Scout and Jem and Dill would have cooked up between schemes to get Boo Radley to come out. Who knows if it will work?

Rethinking Gettysburg

The Gettysburg Address is the best and the most consequential speech in American history. But forcing the nation to war, whether to save the Union, as President Lincoln saw it, or to free the slaves, as history saw it, was a tragic mistake. And although the speech itself is as well crafted as any I can imagine for cementing those goals in place, however mistaken they are, it did so by thoroughly misleading the president's audience and the nation. The deception did indeed herald "a new birth of freedom," but this was not a good thing, because it did so by replacing the idea of freedom as understood by the Founders with its opposite, as understood by President Lincoln. And the nation has been miserable ever since.

The main problem was Lincoln's assertion that the nation was "conceived in liberty and dedicated to the proposition that all men are created equal." While true in a context diametrically different from the one Lincoln wanted his audience to hear, it was most emphatically not true in the context Lincoln implied. Except for "liberty" and "all men are created equal" these were Lincoln's words, not the Founders' words. So when Lincoln says the Civil War was "testing whether that nation or any nation so conceived and so dedicated can long endure"—also Lincoln's words, not the Founders'—he implies the Founders erred in not abolishing slavery at the outset while at the same time using words in our Declaration of Independence that Lincoln cherry picks to make it seem that abolishing slavery was their sole purpose in declaring independence from England and setting up the country. This was wrong; it was not what the Founders did or intended.

While Lincoln flipped the meaning of those words that he cherry-picked from the Declaration, and thus misled his audience, the words he left out were the necessary ones, both on their own and to give correct meaning and context to the words Lincoln quoted. In effect Lincoln implied the Founders wanted to see if a nation set up to abolish slavery could work ("can long endure") without actually abolishing slavery. But by stating the Founders' intent in that way, Lincoln left out entirely what the Founders actually did want to do, as he pointedly passed over the words that described it better than any words ever written—whether in the Declaration of Independence or the Constitution or anywhere else—which was to see if freedom in general could work, by which they meant freedom from coercion by government, whether kings, parliaments, or factions of people who would misuse and manipulate government power to their own ends.

This was no easy task, which the Founders recognized at the time and labored very hard over, both through their written words, such as those in the Declaration and the Constitution, and through the freedom-preserving structure of government that those words were meant to ensure. But while different Founders had different views on slavery and abolition, by the time they settled on the words in the Declaration, there was no thought given to seeing if they could also try to abolish slavery at the same time, if for no other reason than that the American Revolution would have died on the vine if they had tried to bring on that challenge, too. While some Founders had slaves and all were aware that eventually the conflict between their stated ideals and the existence of slavery would have to be addressed, the Declaration from which Lincoln quoted did not state or imply a desire to settle the slavery issue either at the founding or later on, as if the Revolution and the founding of the nation were merely a prelude to the Emancipation Proclamation and Civil War.

The Founders were extraordinarily well read on the philosophies and potential government structures of liberty, and often came across the institution of slavery as a common rhetorical trope to explain what freedom was not. When trying to decide on the relative powers between kings and parliaments, for example, and the appropriate relations between them, it was assumed that the goal was to make sure that men were free, i.e., that they were not slaves.

To be governed by a power that is not "representative" in this sense is to be ruled by an "alien will." It is, quite simply, to be a "slave." If the king cannot be said to represent the people, then his decisions do not reflect their will. If the people cannot act without his permission (that is, if he is licensed to "refuse his assent" to bills passed by their legitimate representatives), they will find themselves in a state of dependence on an alien will—and hence in the condition of slavery. [*The Royalist Revolution: Monarchy and the American Founding*, Eric Nelson, the Belknap Press of Harvard University Press, 2014, Kindle location 308]

Even Alexander Hamilton, our most abolition-minded Founder, was prone to using slavery metaphorically in his writings to rally revolutionary fervor:

He now warned his comrades against "a groveling disposition" that would degrade them "from the rank of freemen to that of slaves." [*Alexander Hamilton*, Ron Chernow, Penguin Books, 2005, Page 71]

My point here is that not only did the Founders have a great familiarity with the structures, theories, and constitutions that might guarantee freedom, the very language in which those debates over government were carried on often referenced the condition of being a slave as the opposite of being free, although this was only as a metaphor rather than an indication that the debates over the nature of freedom and how to preserve it were headed toward abolition. In fact, when Thomas Jefferson tried out some language in the original draft of the Declaration that digressed onto the topic (essentially trying to blame Britain and the slave trade it countenanced in the colonies for our slavery predicament), other Founders objected and it was deleted. Not only was the Declaration of Independence not concerned in any way with abolition or the slavery issue, but this approach to its drafting and signing was entirely consistent with a general agreement among the Founders to avoid the contentions topics of slavery or abolition.

The northern states were not about to override their southern brethren on the slavery issue. All along, the American Revolution had been premised on a tacit bargain that regional conflicts would be subordinated to the need for unity among the states. This understanding dictated that slavery would remain a taboo subject.

[*Alexander Hamilton*, Ron Chernow, Penguin Books, 2005, Page 122]

So when the Founders said in the final version of the Declaration that they signed, "all men are created equal," they did not mean they intended to eliminate slavery. When Lincoln said the nation was "conceived in liberty," as if it were conceived with the principal purpose in mind of eliminating slavery, he was wrong. And when he said the Civil War was "testing whether that nation or any nation so conceived and so dedicated can long endure," he was wrong to imply that the Founders had wanted or expected such a test to occur. In sum, the nation was not conceived in liberty, if by "liberty" a desire to eliminate slavery was meant. And it was not dedicated to any "proposition" at all, much less to one the Founders did not embrace, such as that "all men are created equal," if by that was meant that no slavery would be allowed.

Their purpose in using that powerful phrase in the Declaration, perhaps the most evocative of freedom in the English language, was to make sure it was understood that *all* individuals to whom those words applied were entitled to liberty. Although slaves were not included, this was the key phrase that embedded the concept of the *individual's* right to liberty. By implying that this language covered slaves, Lincoln implied the opposite, as if individuals were not important to the Founders, but slaves as a group, and therefore black people as a race, were. This was totally wrong.

The word "proposition" is a curious one, sounding like something between a theory and a hypothesis. You don't fight wars to "test" whether a proposition or theory or hypothesis is valid; that would be the job of scientific observation or experiments or history to settle. And in any case the language from the Declaration that Lincoln left out, what he skipped over when he substituted the word "proposition," was critical: "We hold these truths to be self evident." They were not propositions, theories or hypotheses; they were "truths," they were "self evident" and they existed because of the "unalienable" (non-severable) rights our Creator endowed us with applying to "all" men, i.e., to each and every man. They were not propositions to be tested in a lab, much less a single proposition to be fought over. And even if they were, the one and only proposition Lincoln posited for testing (a nation devoted to eliminating slavery) was not one the Founders intended.

There are actually five self-evident truths in the Declaration and they necessarily work together to create the freedoms the Founders meant to establish. First, 1) "all men are created equal." Second, each of those men (because "all" men are included) is 2) "endowed by their Creator with certain unalienable (i.e., non-severable) rights, that among these are 3) life, 4) liberty and 5) the pursuit of happiness."

What President Lincoln was apparently trying to establish is some kind of Founders cover for his war, some justification for having embarked on a path of vengeance that would kill 625,000 (the equivalent of six million if adjusted to today's population), including killing or maiming three quarters of the able-bodied men in the South, and so destroy a flourishing economy that it is still backward compared to the North's economy 156 years later.

And "vengeance" *is* the appropriate word. The moral righteousness of the North's mission implies it throughout the Gettysburg Address. When Lincoln reveres "the brave men living and dead who struggled here," the ones about whom the world "will never forget what they did here" or were "these honored dead" from whom "we take increased devotion to that cause for which they gave the last full measure of devotion," he wasn't talking about the men from the South, who were not trying to test the proposition Lincoln posited, or fighting for the cause for which the Union soldiers gave the last full measure of devotion, but fought against it. The soldiers from the Confederacy were often said to be fighting for a "cause," too, but it was not the one Lincoln was referring to at Gettysburg, and there is no hint in his address that they deserved any kind of recognition or reverence such as that which he came to that battlefield to honor the Union soldiers for. His purpose was primarily political, because although the Union soldiers had made great progress, *there was more work to be done.* So to make sure "these men shall not have died in vain," we the living should dedicate ourselves "to the unfinished work which they who fought here have thus far so nobly advanced." Some have said Lincoln honored both sides because he didn't mention either. They are wrong. There was nothing in it for the South other than an implied demand to accept capitulation, dishonor and collapse.

Vengeance is also the intent of the 2nd Inaugural, March 4, 1865, given five weeks before the South's Appomattox surrender (April 9) and six weeks before President Lincoln was assassinated (April 15), which put a sharper point on what the work ahead would entail and why the South deserved to be forced by a righteous North into capitulation, dishonor and collapse.

Fondly do we hope, fervently do we pray, that this mighty scourge of war may speedily pass away. Yet, if God wills that it continue until all the wealth piled by the bondsman's two hundred and fifty years of unrequited toil shall be sunk, and until every drop of blood drawn with the lash shall be paid by another drawn with the sword, as was said three thousand years ago, so still it must be said "the judgments of the Lord are true and righteous altogether."

Although issued in the manner of a threat demanding immediate surrender, these reckonings of the South's sins were, as Lincoln assured us, the true and righteous judgments of the Lord that in spite of Lincoln's blood-for-blood and toil-for-wealth calculations, were of such an innately heinous and incalculable harm that they would certainly survive the ending of the war and leave the South forever in arrears to the black race no matter how much progress might be made by or for them in the future, and no matter how quickly the Confederacy capitulated. These were the kind of debts that no surrender would stop the clock on, that no contrition could atone for, and that no bookkeeping could account for, or so Lincoln seems to say on the Lord's behalf. Although only God would know how much actual wealth was piled or blood was drawn with the lash on those plantations, from Lincoln's practical political perspective, it might as well be infinite, which is what his metaphors imply. With such payback images in the mind of the Civil War's author as it was a month from ending, is it any wonder that reparations and many other forms of retribution and redistribution are still hot topics today and that Black Lives Matter demonstrations still tend so strongly toward violence?

But what has dropped away from the conversation entirely is the notion that black people, as individuals, are entitled to the original Founders' unalienable rights, such as the pursuit of happiness. Now neither blacks nor whites nor women nor men nor transgenders or anyone else is entitled to such individual based rights. Instead government has crushed them in favor of its own power to redistribute outcomes among and between groups. If any one of those individuals wants to freely select his associates, he will be blocked by government's antidiscrimination powers. Thus now all people have been deprived of the rights the Founders meant them to have and instead an all-powerful government is overriding their rights in order to allocate outcomes between groups, an enterprise that only helps government rather than any of the groups it pretends to help.

All the anger we see today is the inevitable result of having abandoned our original freedom to discriminate, which, as I have said, did not depend on any laws or words in our Declaration of Independence or Constitution or anywhere else; it's just the way it was. So when leaders today say "that's not who we are" about attempts to exercise our once assumed rights of discrimination, they are correct, unfortunately. It's who we *were*, but it is no longer who we are. President Lincoln pointed us in a direction directly opposite to that which the Founders did, and the nation is both poorer and headed toward ever more violent catastrophes as a result. While the exact shape of those catastrophes won't be known until they materialize, their general outlines have been obvious since 9/11, and still are.

Underlying this book is a "unified theory" of social organization, one that explains many seemingly disparate mysteries of modern life in America and the world. It explains why all major industries are failing in the degree to which they are governed by antitrust, which includes all the important ones. It explains why the stock market, one of those industries, is no longer producing new companies and economic growth or good jobs, or productivity or inventions. It explains why American children can no longer expect to do better than their parents did. It explains why conservatives are actually the most liberal, indeed socialist, defenders of antitrust, how American principles are undermined rather than supported by "constitutional conservatives," who can't understand what happened to the Constitution or how going back to it is a lost cause. Stated simply, our unified theory says that allowing the freedom to discriminate brings order and harmony while eliminating discrimination causes hate and war, the most important practical example of which is that the War on Terror is the cause of the terrorism it tries to suppress. This was already in the book before 9/11 but was made blindingly obvious by that horrible event that, as everyone said, changed everything.

Or so it seemed. Unfortunately, fifteen years later, not all that much has changed. As bad as President Bush was before and after 9/11, President Obama has been worse, continuing on the same self-destructive path that all of his predecessors traveled down. And so our unified theory is more useful as a guide to what will happen as a result of our studied and determined ignorance rather than a prescription for what to do about it. Even in America, the birthplace of freedom in the modern world, events are driven by tyrannical demagogues in the mold of Abraham Lincoln rather than liberty-loving patriots in the mold of our Founders. The Founders understood the positive consequences of following freedom as our unified theory predicts. While we may hope and pray that something will change to move us in that positive direction again, the theory also points to what will happen if we don't—by far the more likely scenario—and it's not pretty. But as I've said several times now, these things have been obvious since 9/11, and still are. So we'll start there, again.

Speaking of "again," this chapter was finished an hour before I heard the Orlando news. That puts it in roughly the same place the original book was in as the planes struck on 9/11. So, as before, I will make no changes to the text above, and will confine my thoughts on Orlando to these here below. While politicians are again blaming hate and terror, guns and discrimination, the reader by now knows that these lamentable litanies are closer to being the cause of these senseless acts than the basis for a solution to them. Like the original explanation of a video after Benghazi, or the original story that Saddam had WMD, or the original explanation for 9/11 that Muslims hate freedom, these are just reflexive and disingenuous narratives that keep the political class in power that is actually the source of all our problems.

In that vein a few decades ago, there was also the "domino theory" that required us and the Russians to fight proxy wars all over the world to keep the whole world from going communist or capitalist, one of the last and most tragic of which was when this theory justified both Russia's and America's wars in Afghanistan that, between them, led to al Qaeda and, just a few years later, 9/11. The short story is that we supported the mujahideen, the "freedom fighters," against the Russians before the Russians finally quit and went home, and a few years later the freedom fighters turned out to be al Qaeda, and a few years after that, 9/11 happened.

Going back much further, another domino theory was what President Lincoln had in mind with his claim that we had to fight the Civil War in order to keep the whole country from becoming a slave society.

Either the *opponents* of slavery will arrest the further spread of it, and place it where the public mind shall rest in the belief that it is in course of ultimate extinction; or its *advocates* will push it forward, till it shall become alike lawful in *all* the States, *old* as well as *new*—*North* as well as *South*. [Lincoln at Gettysburg:

THE WORDS THAT REMADE AMERICA, Garry Wills, Simon & Schuster, p. 55 [SW 1.426]] [Emphasis in original]

While these justifications for continuous war are not so easy to recognize as political prevarications at the time they are uttered, that is what they are, and it is all that they are. And while my analysis may be hard to take, requiring as it does many adjustments to settled opinion about, for example, discrimination and President Lincoln's place in history, the proof of what I have been saying is piling up. Even CNBC hosts and guests on the Monday after Orlando began to recognize that these events are becoming more frequent. Yes they are. And, I would add, they are getting bigger.

The most popular prevarication of the political class now is still that we have to go after the terrorists "over there" before they come here. But this is really just another version of the domino theory, and it's the excuse President Bush used to justify the War on Terror to begin with. So I will say it again: the War on Terror is the cause of terror, just as our antidiscrimination jihad against "hate" at home is the actual cause of hate. So either we must be prepared to take over the entire world, as Adolf Hitler (who admired Lincoln, by the way) wanted to do, or the backlash against our war will overwhelm us, just as the backlash against Nazi Germany overwhelmed Germany. And either we must be prepared to brainwash every American at home with diversity and inclusion propaganda so that he never hates anyone, or the backlash against the most vulnerable minorities, such as were in that Orlando nightclub, will continue and intensify. Needless to say, I hope we don't go any further down either of these paths, as that will only continue to make things worse, and in any case their practical impossibility is obvious. But if we do, and if the two streams meaningfully merge—the terrorism backlash from abroad and the antidiscrimination backlash at home—as they appeared to begin to do in Orlando, then the real nightmare will begin, which will ultimately involve weapons of mass destruction.

Countdown

Steve Wunsch

Table of Contents

The natural progress of things is for liberty to yield and government to gain ground.

        - Thomas Jefferson

Liberal institutions cease to be liberal[1] as soon as they are attained: later on, there are no worse and no more thorough injurers of freedom than liberal institutions.

        - Friedrich Nietzsche

---

[1] Until some time in the first half of the Twentieth Century, "liberal" was the word most commonly used for what we now call "conservative" or "libertarian." Today, of course, "liberal" means the opposite. That the defenders of freedom and limited Government had the very word that described them stolen by the enemy may speak volumes about the problem that Nietzsche and Jefferson identify. In any case, the terms "liberal" and "conservative" have their modern meanings throughout this text, unless otherwise noted.

September 22, 2001

Preface

The attack on the World Trade Center reminded the world that freedom is why America was founded, and freedom is what our country means to all the people on this planet. But for all our historical attachment to the concept, in recent times we have moved further and further away from the ideal. As this book details, Government intervention to reallocate economic and social outcomes has undermined our infrastructure, set our people against one another, and caused our enemies to proliferate. Not only did this inattention to freedom open us up to the surprise attack on September 11, but the redistributionist ethos that brought us to this pass is pushing us even faster down the same road as we respond to it. As a result we could actually lose this war. Yes, the unthinkable is possible – indeed probable – on our current course.

Although we may still be more free than any other country, the backsliding on our principles must be checked and reversed quickly or we will find it impossible to maintain the moral and political cohesion on which our legitimacy to lead the world fight against terror depends. Moreover, without a return to freedom, the economic infrastructure that enables us to fight will rapidly erode. And most frightening of all, both the number and strength of our enemies will expand without limit unless we stand again for the principles our Founding Fathers enunciated two centuries ago.

With the exception of this Preface and the Afterward, this book was complete on September 10, 2001. The Introduction and the two chapters following it were written in June, July and August, respectively and might be thought of as the unpublished sequel to the various *Auction Countdowns*, Congressional testimonies and letters that I had written over 14 years in my attempt to launch an auction-based stock market. (All are available for download at www.stevewunsch.com.)

While September 11, as everyone says, changed everything, the chief difference with regard to my opinions as expressed herein is a heightened sense of urgency. The reaffirmation of freedom I call for, however difficult it will be, is now a critical and immediate matter of national survival. Consequently, from the title through the last chapter, I have not changed a word since September 10. You will find in the Afterward, however, a brief summary of the international dimensions of the policies I recommend, particularly as they affect our ability to fight terror.

June, 2001

Introduction

The road to hell, they say, is paved with good intentions.

In this book I offer a new perspective on the problem of well-intentioned paternalism, a view I developed in the course of a 14-year effort to launch a market-stabilizing stock auction that came to be called AZX, the Arizona Stock Exchange. Although I didn't start out with an anti-regulatory bent, the experience forced me bit by bit to question the most accepted tenets of regulatory doctrine, first in the stock market, but eventually in virtually every important industry. In the end I became highly skeptical of all Government intervention in private markets.

Perhaps my most surprising finding is that my discovery that America has gone socialist was *not* my most surprising finding. Topping even that one is that *our* version of socialism, which in the end may prove both more durable and more damaging than that which destroyed Russia, is being pursued primarily by *conservatives*. Like Russia's communism, which now seems so obviously idiotic, our country is making philosophical and practical mistakes that will one day be laughed at. Can't happen here, you say? Well, did you think the Soviets said to themselves: Hey, let's adopt a system that will impoverish our people, ruin our respect among nations, turn our great art to mush and make us the laughing stock of the world's philosophers? No. They thought they were following the latest, greatest, most efficient, most fair, economic and political principles. And so do we. We've now got Government experts, supported by the latest, greatest academic theories, designing every major industry and element of our infrastructure. It's difficult, of course, to argue with experts, and virtually impossible to do so industry by industry, detail by detail. So the intervention juggernaut rolls on.

But if you connect the dots in this book, you will spot a pattern others have missed. Competition policy – monopolies, antitrust, patents, etc. – is the hidden driver of all these interventions. It is also both usurping individual freedom and having a profoundly disorganizing effect on our economy. As a result, our most important industries are falling apart. Telecom, electric power, oil, natural gas, air travel, computer software, health care, education and many other critical components of our infrastructure are fragmenting furiously, and most are constantly in crisis and getting worse by the day. Even the stock market, the most important industry in the infrastructure of capitalism, and the one that first clued me in to these problems, is rapidly becoming dysfunctional. You won't need to be an expert in any of the industries discussed to see this pattern. Indeed, it will become clear to you why all the expert attention is the *cause* of the functional disintegration observed.

The situation is far worse than commonly supposed, even by those who think they understand the problems of over-regulation, namely, conservatives. In fact, it is precisely those conservatives who are causing the confusion. Although we Americans consider ourselves immune to socialism by virtue of our freedom-based traditions, we are not. We may have avoided some strains of that virus, like Euro-socialism or the USSR's communism, but the fact is that the plague has mutated around our defenses. It is now carried into our body politic by the very words that once made us immune. Words like "competition," "free markets," "property" and "capitalism" are now used regularly to justify intervention and expropriation in the name of fairness. Antitrust is the Trojan horse that makes such deceptions possible. By providing a *credentialed* excuse for intervention, one with an apparent basis in such laissez faire values as efficiency, freedom and property, antitrust is rapidly leading us to the point where we are agreeing as a nation on *our* version of having "the people own the means of production." On the strength of its false claims, antitrust then lends legitimacy to a virtually unlimited list of other rationales for intervention, almost all of which would – without antitrust – have philosophical difficulty justifying themselves in a capitalist society.

The largely subconscious "logic" by which antitrust provides legitimacy and credibility to the whole interventionist enterprise runs roughly as follows. Since antitrust intrusions are necessary in any case to make sure our capitalist society runs properly (or so they say), it is easy enough to imagine other interventions that Government could undertake to make sure our capitalist society runs *even more* properly. With the big foot of antitrust holding the intervention door wide open, it is exceedingly difficult to deny any other excuse for intervention, although only antitrust can claim to improve capitalism directly. Other programs generally must acknowledge a cost in terms of efficiency lost to red tape or an expense in dollars that must be borne in order to achieve any benefits. Of course the supporters of these programs always argue that the benefits are worth any efficiency cost or dollar expense, and thus attempt to justify them in spite of their costs. But that is very different from being able to claim that there are actually efficiency *gains* to be had from applying the program itself, as antitrust advocates do. Because few dispute this claim, antitrust gets a pass on the standard complaints about big Government.

This is not to say that antitrust is not criticized for its big bureaucracy. But how could we deny its advocates their next expansion – no matter how big the bureaucracy gets – when they can credibly claim that our economy would falter if antitrust were not around to keep prices in check and the paths to innovation and competition open? In other words (if you believe the logic), here is one program that is *not* open to the normal cost-benefit calculation that conservatives tell liberals to subject their programs to. It is difficult to overstate the confidence Big Brother must get from knowing that here is at least one rationale for intervention that *everyone agrees with*. While there is plenty of debate over interpretation and application, there is virtually no visible dissent from the proposition that antitrust is beneficial if properly applied. Since, therefore, virtually everyone agrees that having an antitrust bureaucracy is inevitable, the next logical question is: What else can it do? After all, if Government is needed to prevent businessmen from taking unfair advantage of each other or the public, it is hardly a stretch to imagine Government playing a constructive role re-allocating other economic or social outcomes more fairly, too.

Antitrust's power to justify and inspire intervention beyond its purview is also bolstered by the "national asset" argument – a.k.a.: "its-too-important-to-be-left-to-the-private-market." This argument is most often invoked to attack monopolies providing infrastructure, such as oil, transportation, telecom or the stock market, but is an easily transferable excuse to any program with vocal advocates. Although the argument is connected to antitrust without even the pretense of intellectual rigor, its frequent association with trust-busting, which is presumed to be theoretically sound, makes it easier to swallow confiscations of property for other public purposes, too. If, for example, it is OK to seize "anticompetitive" monopolies without compensating their owners, it becomes easier to imagine taking ranches, too, if doing so would protect a wetland, an endangered species, or some other "public interest." That such uncompensated takings are accomplished by rule rather than forced physical separation does not change the fact that the original owner no longer has use of his property. So what if the rancher was blindsided when the politics changed and the rules changed with them? That is no different than the 180 degree shifts that often cause monopolists' property to be given up to competitors and then, perhaps with a change of administrations or judges, given back or to others. These people are motivated by private greed, not public interest, aren't they? Why *should* we compensate them for taking their property when their motives for keeping it are so impure?

The net effect of all this is that the bureaucratic enterprise, led and legitimized by antitrust, regularly rides roughshod over freedom. That so few of its invasions are commonly recognized for what they are explains both why there is so little concern about them, and why we are so unable to launch an effective counterattack. In large measure this failure to recognize socialism and defend our society against it is due to the fact that conservatives are asleep at the switch as they fiddle endlessly with efforts to perfect antitrust. This is a fool's errand, because, make no mistake, antitrust's apparent intellectual rigor is phony. There is no valid justification whatever for its claims to efficiency or any other alleged benefit. And it is incorrect to claim, as many do – liberal *and* conservative – that antitrust is the least regulatory way to run an economy. Of course, those who make that claim are comparing antitrust either to the presumably more intrusive rate-of-return regulation of utilities, or to full nationalization. And of course those who make such claims are usually doing so in an attempt to burnish their conservative credentials by pontificating on the evils of State planning. But not only are the socialist straw men they deprecate actually *less* interventionist than antitrust, but they are actually *more* efficient. They are less interventionist strictly measured in pounds of bureaucrats needed to administer them, and they are more efficient because they can maintain the network integrity of the industries they administer. In contrast, it is antitrust's mission to bust up and fragment those networks.

Thus conservatives often end up unwittingly pushing socialist approaches that don't work, demonstrating their incompetence on two counts: 1) they are ignorant of the true philosophical content of their own positions, and 2) they are unable to effectively analyze the practical consequences of the remedies they champion. These philosophical and analytical failures are leading to the wholesale adoption of disastrous economic policies, such as "deregulation," and the consequent rapid unwinding of Western economic potential. Worst of all, because of the incompetence of conservatives, the collapsing infrastructure caused by these policies is being blamed on an *excess* of freedom, when it is actually unrecognized socialism that is doing the damage. Why are conservatives making these mistakes? Because, although the falseness of antitrust seems obvious upon inspection, few are doing the inspecting. Perhaps this is due to the fact that those who could do so are, almost without exception, wittingly or unwittingly involved in occupations that depend on Government. Whatever; the philosophical reality today is that, not only are liberals winning politically, but so confused are conservatives that they are doing far more harm to their own cause than the liberals are.

My experience with regulation constituted an accidental and, therefore, a halting and tentative discovery of these problems, which are, in reality, just one problem. Mine is an admittedly outlier view, and deeply pessimistic. The reader may be tempted, therefore, and perhaps justified, to dismiss my claims out of hand. After all, I am not an academic expert even in my own field of stock market structure, much less in the other fields I have come across in an attempt to understand a structurally disintegrating market. My observations do provide, however, consistent explanations for some of the most perplexing developments of our time. From stock market bubbles and crashes to air rage and California blackouts, I think I can explain why so many seemingly unrelated things are going wrong at the same time. Perhaps perversely, I take some comfort in the fact that expert opinion is so consistently at odds with mine. In one field after another, they seem to believe that just a little more patience with the admittedly slow-moving bureaucratic process of identifying and solving problems will yet produce good results. But slowness isn't the problem. Reliance on experts is the problem, because it inevitably blocks private initiative and natural evolution. Having seen close up with stock market regulation how this very process is the *reason* that progress is never made and that disintegration is inevitable, I feel confident that no amount of experts – however brilliant and well-meaning – can solve such problems in any industry. Ironically, if you ask them why communism failed, they will tell you how stupid 5-year plans were, without ever recognizing that they themselves are involved in the same process.

If I am right, implicit in the uniqueness of my view is that none of the remedies espoused by any of the mainstream pundits or politicians – liberals or conservatives, Democrats or Republicans – will do any good. In the absence of a return to the principles of freedom on which this country was founded, the problem of an overweening Government and our consequent decline as a nation will only accelerate. Air travel delays, indifferent service and the risk of crashes will continue getting worse. Blackouts, bankruptcies and rationing will continue to characterize energy delivery. The stock market will continue to get more volatile and less able to raise capital. Health care will continue to frustrate consumers and rise in price. Public education will continue its decline, computer software platforms will further balkanize, phone service will continue to fragment and confuse. And all these and many similar problems will get worse together, feed off each other, and accelerate the decline of our confidence in Liberty. All of these problems will worsen because the only remedies proposed by any of the experts are *political*. That is to say, they seek only to determine which groups will be affected and by how much under the various policy options, with an eye to lining up support for their proposals. What's wrong with that? Many people will tell you that this is how democracy is *supposed* to work. I, for one, don't think so. Consider the minimum wage debate.

Adam Smith viewed the right to sell one's own labor (or to buy someone else's) as the most fundamental form of property he had.[2] But you can listen to a hundred arguments on whether or not to increase the minimum wage, and every one of them will focus only on which groups will be affected and how much by the

---

[2] "The property which every man has in his own labour, as it is the original foundation of all other property, so it is the most sacred and inviolable. The patrimony of a poor man lies in the strength and dexterity of his hands; and to hinder him from employing this strength and dexterity of his hands; and to hinder him from employing this strength and dexterity in what manner he thinks proper without injury to his neighbor is a plain violation of this most sacred property. It is a manifest encroachment upon the just liberty both of the workman and of those who might be disposed to employ him. As it hinders the one from working at what he thinks proper, so it hinders the others from employing whom they think proper. To judge whether he is fit to be employed may surely be trusted to the discretion of the employers whose interest it so much concerns. The affected anxiety of the law-giver lest they should employ an improper person is evidently as impertinent as it is oppressive." Adam Smith, *The Wealth of Nations*, 1776.

various proposals. The "conservatives" try to argue that increasing the minimum wage will harm those at the bottom (thus demonstrating their compassion), while the liberals say not so, and attempt to make a connection between family values and a "living wage" (thus demonstrating their concern for moral issues). Not a single expert will argue that none of that matters. Not a single politician of any stripe will argue that it is fundamentally at odds with Liberty to have Government slicing and dicing every man's property based only on who can muster the votes. Not a single bureaucrat in the Department of Labor will suggest that, perhaps, Government should not be involved at all in setting wages for anyone – regardless of how the groups described in the expert's studies will be affected. And so it is 100% certain that Government will remain in the wage-setting business.

In similar fashion, all of the experts involved in working out solutions to the problems in the industries mentioned above are concerned only with applying the principles of "fairness" – whose ox will be gored if this or that interpretation of the antitrust laws is adopted. Not a single expert or politician of any stripe will suggest that it is none of the Government's business. All will content themselves with trying to wangle an interpretation that favors their own constituents or clients. And everyone will argue that it is only fair – or correct, or efficient, or whatever – to adopt his interpretation. So fluid and vague are the antitrust laws today after a century of conflicting application that the arguments put forward are nothing so much as demonstrations of raw political power. It is ridiculous to think that an efficient outcome will result, much less one based on Liberty. If, as a result largely of the example set by antitrust, the administration of our democracy has now become merely a mechanism for determining which groups have the political clout to take property from others, then the American experiment is indeed over.

I would like to say I have an answer, but that would be unrealistic. The good news is that so many things are going wrong for the same reason, call it the Government Fairness Enterprise, that the solution seems easy: just get rid of it. The bad news is that crafting a politically realistic means of accomplishing that is almost certainly beyond our reach. More likely is the continued extinguishing of freedom's flame, as our aging experiment proves unable to resist the temptation to divide the great big pie that freedom has baked. It may be that we are beyond the stage where, as a nation, we can rejuvenate the experiment by renewing our vows of freedom. It has occurred to me that the phenomena I describe may be nothing more than the natural aging of a successful civilization, the setting in of a certain social sclerosis.

I do, however, offer a suggestion in the final chapter of this book that – while difficult and risky – could allow us to reboot our system. While I suspect my suggestion is as politically unrealistic as the next guy's, I would encourage the reader to consider it seriously, if only to engender thoughts of alternatives. My approach is to ban, in a fairly direct way through a constitutional amendment, the operation of the Government Fairness Enterprise. As such, it would be offensive to almost everyone who benefits from Government – which is to say, all of us. On the other hand, because it would eliminate most of what Government now does, it might be just what the doctor ordered for those who believe we suffer from a Government illegitimacy problem. The question is: Are we willing to give up *all* of what Government can do for us, in return for the opportunity – and burden – of trying to fend for ourselves?

Out of Order

This chapter is about the confusion of conservatives. Government's fairness enterprise – led and legitimized by antitrust – has ignited a full-scale "war of all against all,"[3] as groups press their claims for fair treatment versus other groups. Conservatives are not only not blowing the whistle on this violation of freedom, they are aiding and abetting it. As a consequence, our Government is losing its legitimacy. The violence done regularly in the name of fairness to property rights, individual freedom, Pursuit of Happiness, the Rule of Law and similar descriptors of a just society has gotten completely out of hand. Because conservatives criticize only the details of antitrust, and almost never its basic principles, they have become this new form of socialism's most credible supporters, and the prime reason that the American experiment has lost its way.

When the Sherman Act was passed in 1890, hardly any American economists supported it. A century later the antitrust record is generally acknowledged to include no undisputed successes and many evident failures. But for some reason most modern economists have actually become antitrust hawks, with large majorities of them in surveys conducted between 1976 and 1990 agreeing that "antitrust laws should be enforced vigorously to reduce monopoly power from its current level."[4] How did this transformation occur? And what is the import of the fact that it did occur for the future of antitrust, and for the future of America?

Unfortunately, antitrust's future looks much brighter than America's. Antitrust is causing the rapid functional erosion of every critical aspect of our infrastructure – energy, transportation, telecommunications, education, health care, the stock market, even the mail. In these and many other areas, the failure of

---

[3] Thomas Hobbes, *De Cive*, 1642. In an irony that might have surprised Hobbes, today's "war of every one against every one," as he phrased it in *Leviathan* (1660), is fostered precisely by the all-powerful State he thought would end it.

[4] Paul H. Rubin, "What Do Economists Think about Antitrust?", chapter three in *The Causes and Consequences of Antitrust, The Public-Choice Perspective*, edited by Fred S. McChesney and William F. Shughart II, 1995. The author and the book's editors seem to take comfort in the "statistically significant" decline in the size of majorities supporting the statement between 1976 (85%) and 1990 (62%) as a sign that economists may be waking up to their errors. I don't. The decline merely shows that economists are becoming more sophisticated in shaping their arguments in support of antitrust to realistically include acknowledgement of its imperfections. By so doing, the profession has made it more likely that, regardless of the number that agree with a hawkish statement, the number agreeing that *some* level of antitrust enforcement is appropriate approaches 100%.

antitrust theory to grasp the nature of monopoly has had – and will continue to have – debilitating consequences. This failure is causing us to miss out on potentially huge benefits for consumers; indeed, it is causing benefits we once had to slip from our grasp. It is affecting industries both very old and brand new, both those at the fully regulated end of the spectrum and those on the still forming frontier where it is not yet clear how trustbusters will get their hooks in.

In addition to retarding or dismantling basic economic functionality, antitrust is also inserting a potentially fatal philosophical wedge between our free people and their Government. By cutting us loose from our anchors in freedom and property, antitrust has rendered pointless or worse the fervid debates over how to solve the infrastructure crises. Because almost everyone now accepts at least some form of antitrust virtually without question, those debates will continue to foster socialist solutions that will make matters worse. And they will at the same time continue to corrode our core beliefs by giving the false impression that those failing socialist policies are actually capitalist in nature and democratically chosen. Although I'm still not sure why the views of economists changed from negative to positive on antitrust during a century of antitrust failure, I suspect that the answer lies in the same processes that hoodwinked conservatives, which is the topic of this chapter.

Let me begin with a brief summary of my own views and how I came to them, so that – agree or not – you won't add confusion about them to the general confusion I want to describe. First, I concur with many criticisms made of antitrust by conservatives. For example, I agree that these laws have been so inconsistently applied that their resulting arbitrariness is a major breach in the Rule of Law, perhaps to the point where they could be declared unconstitutionally vague. I also agree that the influence peddling associated with their administration is an unconscionable source of corruption and an irresistible inducement to Government expansion. I, too, recognize that antitrust is driven more by self-interest (of bureaucrats, inefficient competitors, legislators, etc.) than by the public interest its proponents claim. And I agree that our antitrust laws have consistently failed to accomplish even their own competition-enhancement goals. They should be repealed on that basis alone, much less if one also takes account of their massive and invariably negative unintended consequences.

But even as most conservatives level such seemingly withering criticisms at antitrust, the bulk of them are actually coming up with *their own* solutions, how *they* would reform the process, not eliminate it. Deep down, most have come to the conclusion that antitrust's core prohibitions, such as those against price fixing cartels, constitute sound policy. As a result, their criticisms serve only to widen and deepen the support for antitrust. Where I part company with virtually all other conservatives is in my beliefs that 1) *private* monopolies and monopolization are good, not bad and 2), even if they weren't, it is an intolerable violation of freedom to use Government coercion to prevent them. Antitrust could not conceivably do enough good to warrant the massive invasions of property and freedom its implementation requires. Continuing to pretend that this new socialism is actually capitalism will breed more cynicism and hypocrisy than our polity can bear.

A corollary to my views on monopoly and antitrust is that "deregulation" is the *worst* of the options generally acknowledged to be available to policymakers concerned about monopolies. The others – nationalization and rate-of-return regulation of utilities – are likely to produce better economic results than "competition" administered under antitrust. Moreover, they are less bureaucratic, less prone to develop elaborate rent-seeking patterns, less prone to corruption and, because the rules under which they operate are more clear, they are more consistent with the Rule of Law and Liberty. Perhaps most importantly, because they are explicitly socialist in form, their application does not require the pervasive confusion and hypocrisy that antitrust does.

I want to be clear that I am not advocating either of these options. I believe both are at least as inefficient and prone to corruption as their reputations would have it – and that's pretty bad. But deregulation under antitrust oversight is far worse. Because of its arbitrary complexities, antitrust oversight opens the way to far more meddling by bureaucrats, lawyers, politicians, academics, courts and other players in the planning enterprise. It invites Government expansion on an order probably not seen since economists in National Socialist Germany fixed on the inevitability of monopolies as an excuse for the planners to take over. But we have actually one-upped the Nazis. By deciding that *our* natural monopolies can be deregulated under antitrust, we have opened the way for a far more pervasive and intrusive takeover, supported by the propaganda that says deregulation is a laissez faire approach that will make multi-firm competition as coordinated and efficient as a single firm monopoly.

Not only is the efficiency part impossible, but the laissez faire part is a lie. Oversight of the deregulation pipe dream involves many more people than regulation (or nationalization) did, including now teams of antitrust lawyers within each major firm. Indeed, if the planners have their way, all corporate employees will become part of the antitrust enforcement effort.[5] In any case, massive numbers of our most intelligent people within the political, legal, academic and business professions now spend huge and rapidly increasing amounts of time on activities

---

[5] David B. Yoffie and Mary Kwak, Wall Street Journal op-ed, "Microsoft Isn't out of the Woods Yet," July 2, 2001. "With the shadow of future antitrust action hanging over Microsoft's every move, Messrs. Gates and Ballmer must change the company's culture and make antitrust second nature. It won't be enough to give every person a pamphlet and a lecture. Management will have to get *everyone in the organization* to live the right behavior through repeated training, role-playing and drills. Only then will they instinctively do the right thing. In addition, Microsoft has to sweat the small stuff. When it comes to antitrust law, you have to toe the line 100% of the time." [Emphasis added.]

whose only real purpose is antitrust, all of it devoted to this entirely counterproductive and theoretically bankrupt exercise. The wasted or worse energy includes time devoted to devising antitrust-correct business strategies, launching legal and political defenses and offenses based on it, lobbying and advertising for law and rule changes, writing and reading articles and editorials on antitrust, the headlines of which are rapidly approaching more than half of all business news, demonizing and demagogue-ing our most successful and valuable businessmen, and corrupting the focus of academia toward foolish fields that are more harmful than any of the supposedly discredited Marxist, Communist, Socialist, Collectivist philosophies we have rejected. In fact, if you look closely, you will find that antitrust is the modern incarnation of those philosophies, and that its strongest advocates include those who seem surest that we have conclusively rejected them. As a means of co-opting capitalist energies to socialist ends, nothing more efficient has yet been devised by man than antitrust-based deregulation.

Antitrust does not appear as a significant topic in my writing until 1997. I came across it inadvertently, as I was trying to grapple with the surprising realization that what I saw as disastrous stock market regulation was actually quite consistent with antitrust. I had first assumed, along with other critics of the SEC's National Market System (NMS), that stock market regulators had somehow misinterpreted competition policy. In other words, like almost everyone today, I subconsciously agreed with antitrust policy and, therefore, instinctively looked elsewhere for explanations of any problems I perceived. But the more I looked, the more I saw that the problems in the stock market – fragmentation, volatility, free-riding – had analogues in the other industries that were in the news. And the most consistent common element in the stories about all of them was antitrust. So I came to question antitrust itself. Although I am still hardly more than a dilettante on the topic, and only a casual observer of the industries it touches outside the stock market, it is easy enough to see from the similarities across troubled industries that something is seriously wrong with antitrust. It would be an extraordinary coincidence if the obvious correlation between the degree to which industries are in crisis and the degree to which competition policy is applied to them were accidental.

The clincher for me was discovering that the organizing principles of stock markets are *primarily* antitrust violations. That is, stock markets worldwide came into existence *primarily* to violate antitrust (albeit in many cases before its principles were turned into law). When I put this to one antitrust expert, he couldn't imagine it, and averred that stock market cartels were not violations. This much I expected, but his explanation surprised me. As he described it in a series of e-mails, stock market cartels were not violations, because, since they were the only providers of their service (i.e., were monopolies), their output would not exist but for the agreements. Therefore, according to him, they *increased* output, rather than restrained it, and consequently could not be considered anticompetitive. This was an extreme extension, it seemed to me, of the standard argument that supply restraint and monopoly pricing go hand in hand. My expert didn't try to argue that stock markets were not cartels, but merely that they were not harmful on account of the fact that their very existence increased output beyond what would exist without them. So far, he and I were in full agreement. But what about the fact that any output or pricing effects were achieved in the case of stock markets by that evil of evils: the collusive cartel – a "per se" violation?[6] My expert was not concerned, because, even though the colluders may have come together in order to restrain output to raise price, the effect of their having done so was to increase output beyond what would exist without their market. Ergo, they were not anticompetitive. Furthermore – and here's the flying leap of faith, legally – because they were not anticompetitive, they could not possibly be illegal, even though they might be price fixing cartels. I guess by that logic, all a price fixing cartel or a monopoly has to do is make sure that it has a 100% market share and it's off the hook – so much for the per se rule against price fixing.

Cheap shots aside, I wish that my expert had come to my conclusion that the fact that stock markets were good things, even though in form they were basically per se antitrust violations, meant that antitrust had a fundamental flaw. But no such luck. Needless to say, this well meaning and very intelligent expert, well known and often quoted for his knowledge of how antitrust applies in the modern high-tech world, did not move me off my suspicion that antitrust was bunk. And the more I saw the damage it was doing to the stock market, the more I recognized its theories behind the crises in other important industries. And of course the better I understood *those* problems, the more I understood why stock market reforms weren't working. They had all been *causing* problems for decades, not solving them – and there was no end in sight. Quite the contrary: *All* the experts now believe that reforms are necessary in one industry after another. They have become constitutionally incapable of recognizing that reliance on the process of re-forming is why we have the problems they are trying to reform. Surprisingly, I discovered that conservatives are just as susceptible to this philosophical snake oil as the most blatant socialists.

---

[6] "The Congress that enacted the Sherman Act intended to make naked price-fixing agreements illegal per se, and the courts from the beginning have, with only occasional aberrations, faithfully adhered to that policy. A rule of per se illegality for naked agreements not to compete means that no defenses are permitted once the agreement is proved to exist. The judge is foreclosed from considering the appeal of a shorter working day, the hardships visited by competition on small traders and worthy men, or any other value that might arguably be forwarded by the cartel. . . The per se rule against naked price fixing and similar agreements not to compete is the oldest and clearest of antitrust doctrines, and its existence can be explained only by a preference for consumer welfare as the exclusive goal of antitrust." Robert H. Bork, *The Antitrust Paradox; A Policy at War with Itself*, 1978.

While the various "schools" argue the details, no one notices that the arguments about antitrust are only solidifying acceptance of its basic tenets. The Chicago School, the Harvard School, the Virginia School, even my favorite, the Austrian School, bat the issues around endlessly, never realizing that their arguments only give credibility to the notion that antitrust has been fully vetted and agreed on. They are like the schools in those karate movies which compete and sometimes underhandedly wage war on each other, but in the end leave the audience sure of only one thing: karate is cool. Even my own extreme anti-antitrust views have contributed to its acceptance. "Comment" letters I have written to the SEC excoriating NMS have been duly noted as part of the input that the Commission has taken into account when formulating policy. Thus, without refuting or even addressing any of my positions, regulators gain more credibility to pursue ever-greater intervention of the sort I criticize precisely because I criticized their interventions in the comment process.

In truth, I know that no one will ever conclusively prove that antitrust is good or bad or somewhere in between. But that is the strongest argument of all for getting rid of such an interventionist policy. Friedrich Hayek argued that capitalism and freedom were needed precisely because we cannot know enough about the future effects of our interventions to undertake major intrusions. He thought monopolies were fine, even very big ones.[7] On the other hand, in the next breath he also articulates a case for using the power of the State to prevent "aimed discrimination," which sounds remarkably close to modern antitrust theory, such as that used to attack Microsoft and others. Would he recognize, were he still alive, the contradiction between his let-evolution-run view and the current case against Microsoft? Would he see the role played by aimed discrimination in promoting coordination in an economy, or as he preferred to call it, the "catallaxy"?[8] After all, he preferred this new word because it better conveyed the complexity and

---

[7] Friedrich A. Hayek, *Law, Legislation and Liberty*, Vol. 3, *The Political Order of a Free People*, 1979.

[8] Friedrich A. Hayek, *Law, Legislation and Liberty*, Vol. 2, *The Mirage of Social Justice*, 1976. "For a proper understanding of the character of this order [the "market order"] it is essential that we free ourselves of the misleading associations suggested by its usual description as an 'economy'. An economy, in the strict sense of the word in which a household, a farm, or an enterprise can be called economies, consists of a complex of activities by which a given set of means is allocated in accordance with a unitary plan among the competing ends according to their relative importance. The market order serves no such single order of ends. What is commonly called a social or national economy is in this sense not a single economy but a network of many interlaced economies. . . The confusion which has been created by the ambiguity of the word economy is so serious that for our present purposes it seems necessary to confine its use strictly to the original meaning in which it describes a complex of deliberately co-ordinated actions serving a single scale of ends, and to adopt another term to describe the system of numerous interrelated economies which constitute the market order. . . [From] the Greek verb *katallattein* (or *katallassein*) which meant, significantly, not only 'to exchange' but also 'to admit into the community' and 'to change from enemy into friend' . . we can form an English term *catallaxy* which we shall use to describe the order brought about by the mutual adjustment of many individual economies in a market." See also Ludwig von Mises, *Human Action*, 1949, for a discussion of catallactics. In a footnote on page 3, Mises attributes first use of the term to Whately in his *Introductory Lectures on Political Economy*, 1831.

interconnectedness of a society's commercial activities, and the importance of coordination. Would the Nobel laureate who warned us not to go down the road to serfdom have failed to see that using Government coercion to prevent aimed discrimination would push us in exactly that direction?[9]

My point here is that even those most rigorous about freedom can often not resist the temptation to address through their own interventions the screw-ups of the previous ones. Even if there were, bubbling away in the basement of some IO research lab, incontrovertible proof that antitrust is idiocy, I doubt that it would be used to promote freedom by recommending repeal. The discoverer would instead probably turn the idea into a B2B, apply for patents, and use it on some electricity grid somewhere. Don't laugh. That is roughly the story of how we got California's deregulation plan. Power deregulation has been worked on since 1984 by, among others, some members of a think tank now called IFREE (the International Foundation for Research in Experimental Economics).[10] I know of no other think tank with a more conservative philosophy, nor with a more creative approach to exposing the fallacies of State intervention. However, their desire to bring experimenting from the lab to the real world exhibited, it seems to me, the same disregard for the dangers of intervention that the policies they wanted to replace did.[11] Because their work was closely followed by other academics, and was credited with moving deregulation forward, especially outside the Unites States,

---

[9] Friedrich A. Hayek, *The Road to Serfdom*, 1944. Hayek's early classic, perhaps the most passionate and eloquent defense of freedom I have read, nonetheless contains many references to the need for coercion to "create" the conditions in which competition can flourish. As near as I can tell, his willingness to accept "certain kinds of government action" in this regard stems from the following factors. First, Hayek is suspicious that the group actions of labor unions and corporations seem so likely on the historical evidence to involve Government that he has difficulty imagining them remaining private and uncorrupted. Certainly, as he chillingly describes in *The Road to Serfdom*, Hitler's Germany made powerful political use of socialist economic theories regarding the inevitability of monopolies and, therefore, the wisdom of bringing Government in to formally enhance and organize them. Second, Hayek has great respect for the naturally evolved institutions and attitudes that provide us with rules of social interaction, the history and basis for which we have no way of knowing, but which endure because they made us more successful than alternative rules that died out with extinct societies. Antipathy toward monopoly appears to be one such attitude, which may explain why, according to some, it is found in such breeding grounds for freedom as the common law and in some fragmentary comments by Adam Smith. This, in any case, seems to me why he is comfortable with a variety of coercive measures, including enforcement of the prohibitions on "aimed discrimination" that he articulates in Volume Three of *Law, Legislation and Liberty* (1979).

[10] I am on an advisory board for this group, which conducts research and experiments for both scientific and educational purposes. Its principal members have long been associated with the field of "experimental economics," which tests the structures of various market institutions by simulating their incentives with payments to participants in laboratory games. The results are used both to test the efficiency of the various institutions against each other, and to teach students fundamental economic principles, like those of supply and demand. It is hoped that at least some of their research findings will be used to inform and implement conservative policies.

[11] Stephen J. Rassenti, Vernon L. Smith, Bart J. Wilson, "Using Experiments to Inform the Privatization/Deregulation Movement in Electricity," 2001. The centerpiece of their plan is a "decentralized" electronic trading system. Although they were not direct advisors to California, something similar was adopted there. According to the authors, however, California made several mistakes, such as leaving out demand side bidding and flexible time of day pricing, and by allowing hidden non-system trades.

their confidence probably helped convince the doubting-Thomases in California that it was worth a try.

While the IFREE scholars have been sharply critical of some elements of the California approach, they remain convinced that doing deregulation right can still work. If only they meant getting rid of *all* utility regulation, I would agree. But what I fear they do mean is that, if participants were only hitched up to *their* black box, and *their* property rights regime, rather than the ones California used, everything would be all right. I fear this because, even if their approach did "work," that would only further empower the antitrust bureaucracy and the top-down socialist approach to market design. Such an approach replaces normal innovation, competition and evolution with "industrial planning," a process that resembles nothing so much as a perpetual academic audition. However skilled the experts are at their professions, the fact that Government might be using their advice as policy input has nothing to do with freedom, true competition, or capitalism. Mussolini's industrial planning advisors must have been very skilled to make the trains run on time, but it is hard to argue that freedom was thereby advanced, or that those advisors were in any sense conservative. As we have seen in the stock market, replacing a complex and intricately evolved industry with a computerized trading game is not necessarily an improvement. But it does empower the bureaucracy that designs and administers it.

Gridlock

Everyone talks about "the grid." But what is it? The term implies connections to others in a network. Although it seems possible for those others to combine, thus internalizing in a corporate sense whatever physical connections are necessary, no current proposal encourages such combinations, and certainly none would allow a single private owner or trust to connect them all up into a single entity. Instead, we tear our hair out arguing over how to do something else – *anything* else. Conservatives want "greater financial incentives for *independent* companies to own and operate power *grids*."[12] Liberals say "[t]he only way to ensure that we have consumer-friendly policies is to have public control of *the grid*."[13] Governor Davis wants to buy *California's* grid for the people. But what grid are they talking about? If Enron can have its own grid, can I have one in my back yard, supplying my personal power needs and selling any excess from my "co-generator" back to some other grid? Does each state have a grid of its own? Each city? What are "regional grids," and how are the local grids connected (or

---

[12] Industry Standard Magazine, June 26, 2001. Opinion attributed to Kenneth Lay of Enron. [Emphasis added.]

[13] Industry Standard Magazine, June 26, 2001. Quote from Tyson Slocum, senior researcher in Ralph Nader's group, Public Citizen. [Emphasis added.]

not) to them? Why are there multi-state grids in the East and West? Why are they not connected (except poorly) to each other? Why does Texas have its own grid, and why has the Lone Star State's historical policy been to remain *un*-connected to the other grids? Why does Texas have a power surplus, while the Eastern and Western grids are planning for blackouts? Why is the Los Angeles grid not part of the California grid – or is it? How did Los Angeles get to opt out of California's deregulation plan, thus avoiding the blackouts faced by the rest of the state? How did the San Diego grid come to be controlled by a South Carolina company, allegedly enabling it to "shut production units [at San Diego Gas and Electric] in what [two ex-workers] said was an apparent effort to drive up electricity prices [for Californians]"?[14] Can I sell power from my backyard grid to Governor Davis, too, just like Enron? I hear he's paying top dollar.[15] What is THE GRID?

Any such series of questions will pretty quickly lead to the insoluble politics of grid management, and one inescapable conclusion: "grid" is a socialist term. This gritty little word would hardly be needed or used if one entity owned all the power. It is relevant only in the context of *political* control of the production, pricing and allocation of electric power. And its use implies that planning experts will get us out of these perplexing power dilemmas. They don't have much time: by 2008 electric power demand and supply are projected to grow by 19% and 32%, respectively, while the grid's capacity to get the power where it is needed is projected to *decline* by 12%.[16] But, not to worry. Scientists at the Electric Power Research Institute, a non-profit think tank funded by over 1,000 power companies responsible for over 90% of our power, are working on a "blueprint for a radically new conception of the energy grid." What is it? "Turning every car into a roll-your-own generator is just one potential expression of the most radical shift in the emerging business model for energy vending profiled in EPRI's Roadmap: the transformation of passive energy users into freelance energy producers, paralleling developments in interactive media, peer-to-peer file sharing, and self-governance.

---

[14] The New York Times article, "Ex-Workers of Generator Testify on Power Output," June 23, 2001.

[15] The New York Times article, July 19, 2001, "California's New Problem: Sudden Surplus of Energy:" "After months of warnings about power shortages and forced blackouts, an unusually cool July and surprisingly effective conservation efforts have put California in a stunning position: it has so much electricity on its hands that it is selling its surplus into a glutted market. . . . [The] Department of Water Resources, which became the state's main buyer of power after soaring wholesale prices pushed private utilities toward bankruptcy this year, would not provide exact figures on how much the state was selling or how much money it was losing. . . . But the department has said it was paying on average $133 per megawatt-hour this month, much of which it is obliged to buy whether it needs it or not, under long-term contracts signed in recent months. By contrast, officials say, the department at times has sold some of that power back into the market at prices as low as $15 per megawatt-hour. . . . 'This state agency has no expertise in trading,' said Harvey Rosenfield, an official at the Foundation for Taxpayer and Consumer Rights. 'It is amateurish at best and sometimes incompetent, negotiating with a bunch of M.B.A.'s whose goal is to soak California. The state was panicked into leaping into this business, and it is being outwitted.' . . . [Rosenfield added,] "They goofed, and it looks like taxpayer money is being thrown down the toilet."

[16] Industry Standard Magazine, June 26, 2001.

By increasing a sense of ownership in the means of energy production . . ."[17] Great news! My plan to sell energy to Governor Davis is getting better all the time; now I'm thinking I can even plug my car into my backyard grid at night so that I will have even more juice to sell him.[18]

Only problem is – I'm not sure I ever aspired to being an energy producer, freelance or otherwise. And I have no interest in having "a sense of ownership in the means of energy production." EPRI's solution reminds me of one that's been proposed for another industry that's been bugging me. "Everyone knows about the horrors of modern air travel. What almost no one knows is how inventors, entrepreneurs, and government visionaries have teamed up to create new kinds of small planes that can take off and land almost anywhere. 'Escape From Airline Hell' the scenario might be called, and it's coming soon to an airport near you."[19] And, while the government visionaries who can't seem to fix the air travel *grid* are busy dreaming up personal planes for me – with parachutes for the *plane*, no less – visionaries over in the SEC responsible for the stock market's *grid* are coming up with ways for me to be a mini-marketmaker. That's right; I, too, can sell the liquidity represented by my own trades back to Wall Street. All I need is an account at a firm like Cybertrader, whose ads imply that I can trade like Bruce Lee does karate, and I can make money as a day-trader with the big boys.

Well, I have news for all those Government visionaries: I don't care if my personal plane does have its own parachute, or if I do have Bruce Lee's trading system. I don't want to *be* a pilot or a day-trader. And I definitely don't want to be an electric power producer. Even if I did, I would still also want the standard versions of these services without having to become expert enough to co-generate into their grids. For the record, I also don't want to have to become a telecom expert in order to find a phone service that works for me, or become a medical practices expert in order to find a doctor, or a technology expert in order to assemble my own PC operating system. While *some* people may want to do *some*

---

[17] Wired Magazine, "The Energy Web," July, 2001.

[18] I am perhaps too hard on Governor Davis; New York under Governor Pataki is headed in the same dumb direction. The point is made in the following excerpts from a New York Times article, "New York Turns Into a Lab on the Future of Electricity," July 25, 2001. "The New York area, particularly Long Island and New York City, is emerging as a laboratory for new approaches. . . Even the very concepts of supply and demand are getting a second look, as a new state program allows large energy consumers to behave like suppliers, by selling their reduced use of power on the wholesale electricity market. The state government, which had been poised to abandon its historic role of regulating the electricity industry, is playing a huge, if ambiguous, part as both an electricity generator and an investor through its conservation rebates and other incentives." "Last month, Gov. George E. Pataki announced that he would require all state buildings to have at least 20 percent of their electricity supplied by renewable, nonpolluting sources like wind or solar power by 2010." "Many energy company officials have been outraged as the New York Power Authority, a state-chartered agency that supplies power to government and other customers, has built 10 small emergency power plants around New York City this summer. While private companies wait in line for the state to consider their plant proposals — spending millions of dollars in some cases just to complete the preapplication process — the state itself has leapfrogged ahead of them."

[19] The Atlantic Monthly Magazine, "Freedom of the Skies" by James Fallows, June 2001.

of these things, the fact is that the breakdown of these network industries may force *all of us* to learn these skills – or do without an adequate level of their once standard services. It is a deregulatory mantra that choice is an unalloyed good, but that is just nonsense. Rather, the need to engage in unnecessary complexity necessitated by all of these competing choices is becoming one of the greatest frustrations of modern life.[20] Sure, co-generation is possible; Wired magazine says it dates to the Middle Ages. But power was supposed to be one of the standard benefits of modern civilization. What happened?

In a word: socialism. Somewhere along the way to the New Deal, the idea took hold that natural monopolies like electric power must be subjected to rate-of-return regulation. The idea was that natural monopolies would tend so strongly toward monopoly that mere antitrust oversight wouldn't be able to keep the competitors apart. So, the thinking went, just let them consolidate into monopolies, but don't let them gouge. By the latter decades of the 20th century the debate between advocates of these two forms of interventionism gave the impression that antitrust was the closer to pure capitalism. Although this view is entirely false, the antitrust advocates got the ideological upper hand when they styled the imposition of their regime as "deregulation," and went trolling in the last decades of the 20th century for industries that could be "freed" from regulation. So, just as antitrust threw in the towel on pure capitalism at the end of the 19th century, and rate-of-return regulation threw in the towel on antitrust by the middle of the 20th, deregulation threw in the towel on regulation by century's end. Although each new phase represents a ratcheting up of regulation, the latest ratchet to deregulation has been devastating philosophically, because it falsely implies *less* regulation and greater freedom. And, just as the debate between antitrust hawks and doves gives ever greater credibility to antitrust, no matter how successful the doves' arguments are at moving it away from the more draconian applications, the debate between "regulators" and "deregulators" serves primarily to justify ever increasing intervention.

So cowed by the enormity of the power problem are our leaders, and so confused are they when it comes to standing for freedom, that we are now set for the final ratchet. "Regulators Order Formation of Big Grids To Ease Bottlenecks in U.S. Energy Supply."[21] Great: a national grid management system run by the Feds

---

[20] The Wall Street Journal article, "Too Many Choices," April 20, 2001. In a study by Mark Lepper, chairman of Stanford University's psychology department: "Of the shoppers who faced 30 choices, only 3% actually bought jam; of the shoppers who had 6 choices, 30% purchased jam. 'Too much choice is not a good thing,' he concludes. People also feel bad when choosing from a broad selection because they second-guess their pick and worry they have made a poor selection."

[21] The Wall Street Journal article, July 12, 2001. Some excerpts: "the Federal Energy Regulatory Commission ordered the formation of four big electric-transmission organizations to optimize the flow of juice in the Northeast, the Southeast, the Midwest and the West." "The federal orders are intended to jump-start development of electric-transmission organizations that the FERC permitted in a landmark decision called Order 2000, issued in December,

on the same model that is bankrupting California's utilities, and will probably bankrupt California. Whether this phase is called "re-regulation" or "smart" deregulation, the name of the game here is to camouflage increasing intervention with phony free market rhetoric, to pretend that Government is only going to set the rules and provide the level playing field on which the "private" parties will interact. But this phony phraseology is hiding an ugly truth: in reality *this is socialism dismantling our society*. It has happened before, recently to Russia, [22] and long ago to the Roman Empire. [23] Socialism's MO is to use every infrastructure failure as justification for greater interventionism, which of course only produces greater failure. With this process under way, there is no chance whatsoever, no matter what the experts say, that consumers will ever again be happy with electric power service, or the service in any other deregulated industry. Nor will they be satisfied in any industry that goes straight to antitrust regulation without passing through a regulation phase, such as the various technology categories.

The experts will always be optimistic, of course, because instilling confidence in their planning is their path to political power. And their plans are always filled with such complexity that it is not possible to argue with them detail for detail. But listen to the philosophy and it is easy to see why they will fail. And you can also catch the circular reasoning that enables them to see failure as success and, thereby, justify more of it. Listen to Alfred Kahn, for example, President Carter's deregulator of the airline industry and, like his boss, a detail man.[24] In a

---

1999. In that order, the FERC urged the utilities to voluntarily surrender control of their transmission systems to grid organizations that would run daily markets for power and manage the flow of electricity across broad regions. The agency said the nation would benefit from larger, more efficient wholesale-electricity markets, in which transmission owners no longer would be able to favor their own power sales over those of competitors."

[22] The Atlantic Monthly Magazine, "Russia is Finished," May 2001. The article describes "the unstoppable descent of a once great power into social catastrophe and strategic irrelevance." One highlighted quote sums it up: "Russia will soon concern us no more than any third world country. Internal contradictions in Russia's thousand year history have destined it to shrink demographically, weaken economically, and possibly disintegrate territorially." See also Richard Pipes, *Property and Freedom*, 1999, in which he describes Russia's 20th century socialist experiment as the most massive confiscation by Government of private property in history.

[23] Ludwig von Mises, *Human Action*, 1949. Mises basically fingers ancient antitrust for the collapse: "What brought about the decline of the empire and the decay of its civilization was the disintegration of this economic interconnectedness." "It was deemed unfair and immoral to ask for grain, oil, and wine, the staples of these ages, more than the customary prices, and the municipal authorities were quick to check what they considered profiteering. Thus the evolution of an efficient wholesale trade in these commodities was prevented. The policy of *annona*, which was tantamount to a nationalization or a municipalization of the grain trade, aimed at filling in the gaps. But its effects were rather unsatisfactory." "The marvelous civilization of antiquity perished because it did not adjust its moral code and its legal system to the requirements of the market economy."

[24] From a press release for Kahn's 1988 book, *Letting Go: Deregulating the Process of Deregulation, or: Temptation of the Kleptocrats and the Political Economy of Regulatory Disingenuousness*: "Alfred E. Kahn, the Robert Julius Thorne Professor of Political Economy Emeritus at Cornell University and one of the most influential figures in public utility deregulation, says to current regulators: 'Do the bare minimum and then let go.' As the 'father' of airline deregulation when he was chair of the Civil Aeronautics Board from 1977 to 1978, and the author of the landmark two-volume set *The Economics of Regulation*, Kahn applies his experience and perspective to

July, 2001 letter to the editor, this consummate expert on the industry and deregulation explains his delight at the Justice Department decision to appeal its loss of a predatory pricing suit against American Airlines. In essence he argues for stricter antitrust enforcement as the necessary condition for deregulation to work. Kahn continues to insist that there are only two ways to run the industry: regulation or deregulation (i.e., under antitrust). [25] Obviously Kahn prefers deregulation, apparently because he has bought the propaganda about it being the less regulatory option. It is impossible to argue with his expertise, and he makes a good case that American did engage in predatory behavior. But his blind assumption that too little competition is the problem, rather than too much, is frightening. Typical of today's regulators and academics, he is absolutely incapable of seeing that worrying about such things as preventing predation or monopoly may be precisely why the industry, two decades after he deregulated it, has taken a shape that consumers find revolting. This is scary, because the evidence of industry failure is clear to everyone who flies, presumably including Professor Kahn. How can he miss it? The answer appears to be that he is so buried in competition argot and self-referential regulatory assumptions about the efficacy and efficiency of competition that he is blind to the misery it is causing. He is blind to the possibility that true efficiency and true competition might be better served by just letting the network monopoly form naturally.

Why is it that economists are the only consumers who can't see that deregulation has been disastrous? Perhaps economists have a greater ability to be patient, to give competition a chance to solve any service disruption or confusion problems. In any case, consumers not steeped in competition theory are not so patient. They are more likely to see service declines as the consequence of any proximate Government action, like deregulation, and are less likely to be willing to wait for theory to produce results. I know many ordinary people (i.e., non-economists) who are frustrated not just with air travel, but with telephones and many other modern marvels, like computers and Internet service. Often they will spontaneously express outrage at the breakup of AT&T or anger at what the Government is doing, or not doing, with airlines. Funny thing, though, the economists I know generally think deregulation has been successful. They point to such facts as the decline in long distance phone rates or airline ticket prices as

---

evaluating the regulatory process and policies now transforming the telecommunications and electric power industries. He shows how current regulatory efforts are biased toward producing immediate results and offers concrete suggestions on how to deregulate for optimal long term success."

[25] Letter to Wall Street Journal, "Airlines Need Freedom Of Competitive Entry," by Alfred E. Kahn, July 12, 2001. "The standard economic test of whether the latter, demand-inelastic customers, are being exploited is whether the charges to them exceed the costs of serving them alone. There are *only two ways* of ensuring that that stand-alone limit is not exceeded. One would be by direct *regulation* of the fare differentials – which we properly abandoned 23 years ago. The other, the only one consistent with *deregulation*, is freedom of competitive entry." [Emphasis added.]

proof that the competition has been healthy. But hasn't service gone down, too? They don't see it. Their belief in competition and, if necessary, Government action to enforce it, apparently overrides any disappointment they might otherwise feel as consumers with the services they use.

But there is another funny thing: Those economists who supposedly believe in the importance of free markets to provide price signals don't appear at all concerned that Government action may be the primary cause of suppressed or spiking or otherwise distorted prices in deregulated industries. Could these interventions be encouraging energy price pirates, or causing the frequently profitless operation and sometimes bankruptcies of utilities and airlines? No, of course not; that's the way the free market works, don't you see? If you get the impression that I think economists are being disingenuous when it comes to observing the industries they are expert about, that would be a reasonable assumption, but it would be wrong. The funniest thing of all is that I find economists to be entirely sincere in their evaluations of these situations. But this fact is also the scariest of all. It means that, like in a science fiction movie, economists appear to have been abducted by alien antitrust monsters that have re-wired their brains so that they can no longer see anything that does not confirm their positive views on antitrust.

The electric power industry is the most visible of today's deregulation disasters, but its problems so far only include a few blackouts, price spikes and utility bankruptcies. Though bad enough already, things will get much worse when the consumer also has to deal seriously with the "opportunity" to "shop for power," as New York's Con Ed urges in an advertisement.[26] It is hard to imagine that Con Ed actually thinks consumers will look forward to comparing power suppliers. In any case, the primary purpose of the ad, it seems, is to enable the utility to make clear that it has no responsibility for the price of power, only for its delivery, which, according to a big pie chart, only makes up 35% of the delivered price.

This is typical of every deregulated industry: responsibility for the overall product is diverse, confusing and influenced heavily by Government. In fact, if you were to apportion responsibility for the overall value propositions embodied by air travel, utilities, telephone service etc., you would probably come out with an amorphous Government role responsible for over 50% of the value, and perhaps over 90%, in all of them. This means that the "competition" intended to serve consumers has only small and shrinking portions of the consumer experience to play with. The rest is Government's responsibility, and the consumer's problem.

---

[26] An excerpt from the ad on p. A25B of the Wall Street Journal, July 9, 2001, reads: "Through the Power Your Way program, you can now buy electricity and gas supply directly from the energy services company (ESCO) of your choice. Shop around for savings, evaluate various ESCO offers, compare prices and find the energy supplier that best meets your needs."

And Government's proportionate role grows with every new initiative by the planners to commons-ize the practices or competitive positions of the players. With every requirement that a phone company give "reasonable" access to its network to the competition, or that a software company allow its competitors' products to be sold alongside its own – or disallowed from tying its own products together – Government's role grows. Whether the role is achieved by behavioral mandates affecting "private" competitors, or, when that fails to produce a sufficiently "public interest" attitude, nationalization of "essential facilities," the heavy hand of Government controls increasingly dominant portions of the value proposition in every major product or service. This marginalizes the value to the consumer of any "competition" that can be trumped up, and puts meaningful service improvements permanently beyond the reach of anyone. Air travel congestion problems, for example, now appear insoluble except through "national consensus" on how to address the issues. [27]

Thus it is that antitrust treats competition itself as a commons. Just as we need rules to prevent fishermen (in the classic example) from over-fishing the sea until all the fish are gone, we need antitrust to preserve our competition resource. This kind of thinking goes much deeper than the ordinary it's-too-important-to-be-left-to-the-private-market rationale, which sees important industries referred to by such commons-like terms as "national asset" or "essential facility" in order to authorize regulators' ministrations. Here, the process of competition, itself, in each industry and generally, is the commons. Without antitrust, the competitors would combine or kill each other off. In one sense, this analysis is accurate, at least for network industries. Natural monopolies are called what they are precisely because this would, indeed, occur most of the time. What the antitrust theorists are missing,

---

[27] "But industry experts say the public remains dissatisfied, still acutely conscious of delays. And the Air Transport Association, the trade group for the major airlines, is trying to shift attention away from calls for Congress to enact a 'passenger bill of rights,' and toward creating a national consensus for new runway construction. The airlines see that step as crucial to improving their on- time records in the years ahead, as air traffic continues to grow. The airlines and the controllers' union, the National Air Traffic Controllers Association, are drafting a letter to President Bush seeking a strong statement from him that building new runways is a national priority. John M. Meenan, vice president of the Air Transport Association, said the airlines would like Congress to create incentives for local and state governments, where authority for runway construction typically rests, to pay attention to the needs of the carriers and their passengers. One method, Mr. Meenan said, would be to threaten loss of federal highway funds for cities that will not build new runways that Washington thinks are needed. The controllers' union and the Air Transport Association will sponsor what they call a 'summit meeting' here on Thursday that will include an unusually broad group, including the biggest union of airline pilots and organizations representing airports, regional airlines, cargo airlines, owners of private airplanes and business airplanes, and aerospace manufacturers. The F.A.A. administrator, Jane F. Garvey, will give a speech praising the cooperation that has helped reduce delays this year, a spokesman for the agency said." The New York Times article, "As Flight Delays Ease Off, New-Runway Push Begins," July 26, 2001. It is doubtful that Ms. Garvey's speech will mention that, if "cooperation, which now includes conference calls every hour among the airlines and air traffic control headquarters, has played a role in easing delays," then an obvious solution to delay problems is to allow natural consolidation of the airlines by getting rid of antitrust laws.

however, is that such a result is integral to normal Darwinian competition. That is, such consolidating competition is integral to the process by which the economic infrastructure molds and remolds itself in constant response to what consumers want. Preventing such competition can only bring disorganization and disastrous service to consumers.

Taking air travel again as an example, the basics of flying also include getting your ticket through a travel agent or the Internet (or shopping around enough to know when it's safe to get it directly from an airline), getting to and being in airports, relying on unappetizing food in the air and on the ground, getting your luggage through the maze of often incompatible luggage handling services, getting the air traffic control system not to bottleneck your flight, and hoping it won't crash.[28] Your carrier has almost no control over most of these services, and little financial incentive to improve the ones it does control. In fact, quite the opposite: Your carrier will benefit in the degree to which it lets *other* carriers do the heavy lifting on designing, test-marketing and providing any common services. And on services that would be theirs alone initially, such as roomier seats, olives in salads, better safety maintenance, or better ads about safety maintenance, competitors would soon copy any successful ones, making the airlines that spent the bucks up front feel like fools, and their shareholders the poorer as their competitors get a free ride on their R&D expenditures. After all, most of the value proposition in the air travel experience is an un-differentiable commodity: Every airline is pretty much the same when it comes to time in the air, and they all get you from one place to another. Not only does this mean that it will do you no good to blame your particular carrier for a problem, but it means that none of its competitors have any incentive to do any better, no matter what their ads say. Any improvements will be copied by competitors, and will be attributed by consumers to the general field, anyway, rather than to the individual company that spent the money to experiment with the improvement. Loyalty to any of the competitors

---

[28] It is clear that competition and antitrust generally are significant drivers of danger in the skies. The primary problems are: 1) sloppy maintenance on the part of small or new airlines with little reputation stake to protect and a strong financial incentive to deliver cut-rate fares [The Wall Street Journal article, "Alaska Air Crash Probe Unearths Lapses in U.S. Design, Maintenance Regulation"], 2) the competitive pressure on all airlines to take off even in bad weather [The Wall Street Journal article, "Cold Calculation: Trial of a Sacked Pilot Offers Inside Look At Airlines Safety"], 3) the congestion that results from airlines listing more routes than can possibly take off on time just to keep the competition from listing those routes – such congestion leads to sometimes dangerous behavior on the part of outraged consumers, and higher chances of collisions in the sky and on the ground, 4) a flight coordination problem that is many times worse for the multiplicity of competing airlines than it would be for a few or one, and is clearly beyond the capacity of the Government's air traffic control system to handle, 5) bureaucratic bungling and jealousies that prevent the adoption of simple and cheap radar systems, the lack of which has resulted in numerous in-air collisions and deaths involving small planes from commuter airports [The Wall Street Journal article, "Lost Horizons; Small Airports Covet Cheap Radar System, But the FAA Bars It; Midair Collisions Don't Sway Agency, Which Supports A Costly New Technology," July 16, 2001]. All of these problems would be minimized if airline consolidation were allowed, such that a monopoly (or a cooperative cartel) could emerge with a reputation stake in safe, efficient and convenient air travel.

under these conditions is fleeting and, ultimately, absurd. So why would anyone but an economist expect deregulation to improve service? They wouldn't.

And then there are the difficulties of coordinating any particular industry's service with those of the other industries of the catallaxy. Just add to the problems described above for airlines the impossible task of improving service when the industry is local, regional, national, and international in scope, providing infinite opportunities for parochial rivalries among regulatory jurisdictions to fragment the overall network. In electric power, for example, there are a large number of competing jurisdictions controlling the grid(s), particularly because there are also a large number of competing inputs to its product, such as coal, oil, natural gas, nuclear, solar, wind etc., many of which are also subject separately to utility regulation or antitrust, and can come from near or far. And those inputs also have other potential uses that compete with electric power generation. Furthermore, just as they have many competing *inputs to* their product, electric power generators also have many competing *users of* their product, such as those now lobbying Sacramento for special treatment on blackouts.[29] And power is just one component of the energy industry, every other element of which is also in constant crisis due to the same interventionist policies that plague power.

Apparently, antitrust economists have concluded en masse that converting the bulk of the responsibility for basic services into a competition commons is a viable plan. But what are they thinking? Marxist planners might imagine they could sort through such tangles, but we're talking here about free-market capitalists. The very philosophy they espouse has as its central tenet the impossibility of the planning they are engaged in. As far as I can see, the antitrust-alien-abduction explanation is the only realistic contender. There is just no other way to explain how people who believe in limited Government and freedom could possibly conclude that letting Government be responsible for the bulk of service in the most important industries, let alone having them all coordinate efficiently with each other, is either a good idea, or consistent with freedom. But here it is. Almost all economists appear to buy into the notion that Government should commons-ize

---

[29] In an illustrative twist, Chevron, a supplier of one of those inputs, warned the State that, unless it were exempt from blackouts, it would reduce refining production in California. This might not only complicate the task of securing fuel oil as an electric power input, but could also cause gasoline and jet fuel prices in the State to soar. While Chevron's case sounds compelling, the problem of trying to manage the catallaxy through political processes is complicated by the fact that there are many other applicants for exemptions. "Citrus farms, amusement parks and even tatoo parlors are among the 6,500 businesses that have applied for special status from the PUC." In addition, Chevron, by its own admission, does not meet the PUC's criteria for exemption, namely that the business would "present 'imminent danger to public health or safety' " if it lost power in a blackout. Wall Street Journal article, "Chevron Warns California About Effects of Blackouts", June 6, 2001. Two days later (June 8, 2001) an article in the New York Times put the number of supplicants for exemptions from blackouts at 10,000.

almost all the big industries through antitrust.[30] Although they think they are promoting competition, they are actually destroying it, at least in a Darwinian sense. Their "competitions" are actually more akin to intramural volleyball tournaments, or to forcing the world's armies to break up into a hundred thousand soccer teams – one struggles to come up with a sufficiently derisive analogy to capture the utter foolishness of the exercise.

One sign of the ridiculousness of antitrust is how the most respected antitrust leaders puff up in full self-righteous regalia to announce – or denounce, as the case may be – diametrically opposite interpretations of the laws. A great example occurred in the wake of the failed GE/Honeywell merger, which was approved by the U.S., but blocked by the E.U. Amidst all the finger pointing across the Atlantic, on our side of it only Laura Tyson (former chief economic advisor to President Clinton, and dean of the Haas School of Business at UC Berkeley) recognized that both Mario Monti's position and ours were based on "reasonable legal and economic arguments."[31] Ms. Tyson then goes on to call for international harmonization of antitrust laws, a position taken now by both Clinton and Bush antitrust chiefs, and a seemingly reasonable and even urgent one, given that 80 countries have now copied our idea and have their own versions of such laws. But how in the world will we achieve global harmonization when we can't even achieve it here between the various federal and state antitrust authorities, or from one administration to the next?

And even if we could adopt a single view, that would just give greater confidence to the planners in their hubris. The negative effects of antitrust described above would exist even if there were a single approach that everyone agreed on, because it is not primarily the flawed application of antitrust theory that is the problem, but its foolishness to begin with. It is critical to realize this. Antitrust must be evaluated on its merits and rejected outright for cause. Not because it is inconsistent in application. Not because there are disputes about it. Not because bureaucrats are self-interested or even corrupt. We must reject it because, even in its purest form, it is bad policy. Unless we do this, the debates over how to reform it will do nothing but strengthen adherence to it, without ever resolving their conflicts. Indeed, as we will see below, the irresolvable and inevitably proliferating conflicts over interpretation provide the primary fuel for the juggernaut. While every antitrust school, and especially the conservatives in them, revel in pointing out the inconsistencies, they all implicitly have an ideal

---

[30] Actually it's not just big industries they go after; some of the industries they find in need of their competition ministrations include, according to University of Mississippi economist William F. Shughart II, "high-priced, non-ethnic frozen entrees"; "noncarbonated, ready to serve, naturally or artificially flavored fruit drinks, fruit punches, or fruit ades which contain 50 percent or less fruit juice and are customarily sold under refrigeration to the consumer"; "direct contract front-loaded trash removal in Dallas." Quoted in James V. DeLong, CEI's 1997 *Antitrust Reader*.

[31] New York Times op-ed, "The New Laws of Nations," July 14, 2001.

interpretation. In spite of, or more correctly, because of, the endless striving for these false ideals, antitrust and the Government growth it sustains can only increase until it destroys our society.

The only way to truly drive a stake through the heart of a socialism like antitrust is for a free people to resolve firmly to adhere to libertarian principles and discover that those principles are inconsistent with it no matter what the theorists say. Such resolve must be strong enough to reject even policies that, as far as we can tell, *would* improve our lives, if we discover that they would violate such principles as freedom, property, or the Rule of Law. To remain free, we simply must be willing to forego potential improvements, even those that no one can see any problems with. Now, I believe that freedom will produce the most satisfactory society anyway, and that doing without potential improvements that are inconsistent with it will not really result in any loss. I also believe that America was uniquely founded on that belief and, if she is to survive, will need to return to it. I will explore some explicit ideas toward that end in the next chapter. Next, however, let's look more closely into some of the antitrust theories that best illustrate both the violation of freedom required for their implementation and the theoretical fallacies underlying their failures in practice.

Blind Spots

Although the choice between antitrust regulation and rate-of-return regulation springs from a false dichotomy,[32] its effects are very real, for two reasons. First, because Government is always empowered by the opportunity to make arbitrary decisions, getting to make the phony judgement call – is it or isn't it a natural monopoly? – enhances Government power. Second, while the distinctions may be arbitrary to begin with, once subjected to one regime or another, the initially arbitrary regulatory choice creates distortions that lead to real differences pretty quickly. The divided territories resulting from separate regulatory fiefdoms under rate-of-return oversight, for example, make it exceedingly difficult to throw industries like electric power or telecom back into the wilds of competition. This is especially so if our expectations of ideal deregulated behavior are shaped by naïve antitrust concepts, like "perfect competition."

Trying to turn discreet local monopoly territories developed under rate-of-return regulation into perfect competitions will never work, and would lead to horrible results if it did. Incumbents will never give up their advantages, not even for the right to raid some other incumbent's territory. Knowing the value of

---

[32] That the choice is, indeed, based on a false distinction is hardly doubted anymore by anybody. In fact, the whole deregulation movement could be thought of as springing from a recognition that the dichotomy was false all along. Now the thinking is that we can just subject *all* of these industries to antitrust, even if they are natural monopolies.

monopolies, they are not so stupid as to think such raids would succeed or be worth the risk of leaving the home territory undefended. Regulators are another story. That time after time they have fallen for such naïve plans in industries like telecom and power, and are always surprised when they don't work, demonstrates with absolute clarity that they haven't a clue about the basic nature of the beast they are regulating. It should come as no surprise, then, that neither do they have a clue about the needs of the consumers on whose behalf they think up these inane schemes. The bureaucrats push these solutions, *as if there were no consumer benefit to consolidation and standardization across territories, and as if they could restrain the natural consolidation instincts of the deregulated competitors without undue coercion.*

The furies unleashed by the Telecommunications Act of 1996 are a case in point. Introduced with much fanfare and excitement over the coming benefits of competition, the Act elicited a boom in telecom stocks, especially new ones who figured that all the customers were up for grabs. With the Baby Bells being enticed out of their "last mile" monopolies by the prospect of entering the long distance business – the regulators' quid pro quo – it looked like everyone had a great new business to get excited about. The consequent investment boom sucked in both old and new telcos and was both much larger than – and perhaps the main driver of – the more visible dot-com bubble. In any case, telecom market cap had dropped $1.7 trillion by July, 2001 since peaking at $2.7 trillion in March, 2000. That loss eclipsed by far the damage done to stock investors by the bursting dot-com bubble,[33] and it looks like much of the $120 billion in junk debt issued to push the boom along will add insult to injury. The fundamental flaw in the regulators' grand scheme is the idea that more than one network is needed or desired. This led Wall Street and Main Street investors down the Primrose Path of believing that all of these hopeful companies could reap huge profits by connecting and servicing telecom needs. The problem, however, was the relatively fixed number of telecom customers. [34] The New York Times puts it succinctly in an article about one fiber optics networker:

---

[33] The telecom stocks accounted "for more than 90% of the net loss in stock wealth in that period." The Wall Street Journal front page article, "Downed Lines; Telecom Sector's Bust Reverberates Loudly Across the Economy; Impact on Jobs and Investors is Proving Much Bigger Than That of Dot-Coms," July 25, 2001.

[34] "The endgame for these companies was always to sell out. Nobody was looking to run a telecom services company 15 years down the line. The money allowed companies to go out and build networks and go after customers in competition with the old-line telecom companies, which had networks that were 30 to 40 years old. The argument of the New Economy companies was that the Old Economy companies had the customers and the revenue base, but they didn't have the networks. The new guys said, 'We can borrow money from the markets, build out the networks and then sell to the guys who have the customers'. . . A couple of things caused the endgame to fall apart. . . First, the big guys started consolidating. So, among the long-distance carriers and the Baby Bells, you came down from about 13 companies to seven. So, the number of potential buyers sharply contracted. And second, they borrowed more money to do this. . . Suddenly all these costs became a reality, and the bond market fell apart. . . It

"In recent years, Corning executives spent about $10 billion acquiring other companies in an effort to grab more of the fast-growing telecommunications business. But over the last year, investors and executives decided that the industry had overreached and that many of the new communications networks might never be used. Financing quickly dried up, and Corning found itself with fewer customers." [35]

And what about those last mile monopolies the regulators were trying to quid-pro-quo the Baby Bells out of? Well they're still standing, and are the only component of the telecom universe that still has both pricing power and an ongoing business. That may change, since they are also still a great source of competition complaints. [36] Totally frustrated with attempts to get the Bells to provide equal access to their networks to competitors, such as other Internet Service Providers, the talk now is increasingly of forcing the breakup of the Baby Bells, too, so they can't discriminate in favor of their own ISPs. With the stub of the old AT&T now clearly in the final stages of disintegration, perhaps now would be a good time to sit back and assess the damage to the whole concept of telecommunications that this bust-up and break-up policy has produced. Especially since competition is clearly the reason the U.S. lags so far behind even socialist Europe, with its administered standards monopoly, in developing cellphone services.[37]

From the consumer's perspective, all this regulatory maneuvering would be a big bust even without the accidental stock market bubbles. That is because the condition regulators are trying to prevent is the very condition consumers want: a consolidated network under common or at least cooperative ownership. While *intra*-industry competition may indeed disappear if a monopoly is allowed to form, that is no loss from the consumer's perspective, because such competition only degrades the network he seeks in terms of functionality, and increases its cost. And such intra-industry competition will die out only if the consumer's interest is served better by that network monopoly than by other services he could spend his

---

became apparent that the ability of the potential Old Economy buyers to take over the debt of the new companies had substantially deteriorated in the past three years." The Street.com Interview with Ravi Suria, April 2, 2001.

[35] The New York Times article, "Second-Quarter Loss Hits $4.76 Billion at Corning," July 26, 2001.

[36] The New York Times article, "Group Is Said to Accuse Pacific Bell of Monopoly," July 26, 2001.

[37] The Wall Street Journal article, "That *%&#)@* Cellphone!" July 23, 2001. "Many customers wonder why service in the U.S. isn't as reliable and seamless as in many other countries. One reason is that the U.S. system is a hodgepodge of different technologies and competing carriers. In contrast to the unified technology used in Europe, for instance, U.S. carriers employ several incompatible setups. It stems from the fact that the U.S. government let phone companies go their own ways. The result is that most phones need to work on two or even three different network systems. A user who places a call on a modern digital signal can end up being flipped to an old-fashioned, scratchy analog signal, or to a different flavor of digital. Maintaining so many technologies adds to the complexity and cost of providing adequate calling capacity in each community."

money on. Indeed, *inter*-industry competition – often monopoly versus monopoly – is the most important kind of competition there is in terms of true consumer interests. It is the only kind of competition by the process of which the consumer's preferences can fully play out in such a way as to meaningfully change his environment for the better. Or, more correctly stated in Darwinian terms, his preferences are the environment in which products compete to find niches and to survive. The more complex the economy becomes, the more likely it is that the most powerful competitors will be networks.

That regulators are preventing this very competition is a travesty. Fostering permanent intra-industry competition prevents network industries from developing their full strength, although their appeal even in much-weakened form is evident. No one wants to go back to having *no* power, *no* planes, *no* phones, and *no* computers. But these network monopoly competitors are clearly underperforming drastically relative to their potential. This is the cause of all the rage, hearings, and Bills of Rights swirling around the infrastructure industries. In short, a consumer revolt is brewing. While it is yet inarticulate and unsure of exactly what it is revolting against, it is becoming clear that neither regulators nor deregulators are the consumer's friend (and wait 'til you see what they think of *re*-regulators). While consumers cannot be expected to decipher all the complex and contentious antitrust theorizing (not that there is anything there really worth deciphering), the one obvious thing is that somehow all this gobbledygook gives Government the responsibility for the quality of these vital services. And, because Government has taken it upon itself, via antitrust, to run these important networks, the dissatisfaction could coalesce into a more general discontent with a Government that will increasingly be viewed as illegitimate.

That conservative economists are missing the network boat is extraordinary. To do so they not only have to ignore the implications of Hayek's and Mises' (admittedly esoteric) catallaxy, but they also have to miss the obvious implications of such mundane concepts as *division of labor* and *comparative advantage*. Does the former only refer to individual workers getting better at the manual tasks they specialize in? Does the latter only refer to nations specializing where they have natural or learned advantages? Don't economists see that companies, groups of companies, and industries do the same thing? They *specialize* at what gives them their best shot. Monopolies and networks are the natural result of the same process that economists love to praise in workers and nations when they talk about the sources of efficiency and productivity. Why not extend the concept? Why blast monopolies for creating those "dead weight loss" triangles, as though they were Bermuda triangles where output mysteriously disappears? With all due respect to their neat little graphs, the enhanced productivity that could result from better coordination of the catallaxy's various components could easily produce *greater* output in the presence of monopolization, not less. Where did this idea come from that "efficient" utilization of a nation's resources requires that each and every business in it run flat out all the time, and always "arms length" separate from all the others? Bodybuilders, who build up every muscle individually with exercises targeted at stressing it to the max, don't win races or any other Olympic events, because their bodies are inefficient at such specialized tasks. While each muscle may be very strong, getting them all to work together efficiently to run, throw, slide into a base, or do any other complexly coordinated action is out of their league.

Since all economists have bought into the multiple-arms-length-companies-running-flat-out-all-the-time approach to full employment, they have completely ignored any benefits that might come from any other approach. For example, wouldn't a monopolist restraining supply of his product have the effect of relieving scarcities in the inputs to it, thereby releasing them for other uses? Wouldn't this have the effect of husbanding scarce resources, both of the monopoly product and of the inputs to it, and foster better stewardship as a result? (This is equivalent to the pitcher conserving and coordinating energy for that fastball, relaxing all unneeded muscles so that those necessary to the task will be able to do the job, as opposed to the bodybuilder who stands before the judges simultaneously flexing every single muscle.) Wouldn't there at least be *some* benefits to cooperation among competitors, predatory monopolization, or price fixing? Doesn't better coordination matter at all? How about better compatibility, better standardization, better price signals, more energetic capital, more faith in capitalism – or *something*?

All economic experts were blindsided both by the productivity gains of the late 'Nineties and by the associated economic strength made possible by the non-inflationary growth that better productivity enabled. They are now equally surprised to find both productivity and growth disappearing together. One possible explanation is that, for a while, the techies had the run of the economy (or catallaxy, whatever) before the trustbusters could figure out what they were doing. So, relatively unrestrained monopolization led to productivity miracles. Now the cops have caught up and the experts are re-forming each violative situation separately, company by company, industry by industry, state by state, agency by agency. No wonder things are getting gummed up. Isn't it just possible that economists are missing a major, perhaps *the* major, contributor to productivity? Just as productivity comes from better intra-company coordination processes, isn't it possible that the inter-company and inter-industry coordination fostered by monopolization is a key to greater productivity, too?

Fooling Freedom

How did conservatives – and conservatives in America, no less – get sucked in to such false theories? It may help to consider how good intentions have played out historically in the debate between freedom and socialism. Today there is virtually no opposition to the notion that, *if properly applied*, antitrust is beneficial, even necessary. So, while there is no reason yet to doubt anyone's good intentions, we would do well to worry that such unanimity of self-interested opinion has fixed on a theory that requires massive Government coercion. And we should keep in mind that, if these seemingly freedom-based theories turn out to be false, it won't be the first time that freedom has been fooled. According to Mises in 1972:

> "It is a fact that a hundred years ago only a few people anticipated the overpowering momentum which the antilibertarian ideas were destined to acquire in a very short time. The ideal of liberty seemed to be so firmly rooted that everybody thought that no reactionary movement could ever succeed in eradicating it. It is true, it would have been a hopeless venture to attack freedom openly and to advocate unfeignedly a return to subjection and bondage. But antiliberalism got hold of peoples' minds camouflaged as superliberalism, as the fulfillment and consummation of the very ideas of freedom and liberty. It came disguised as socialism and central planning. No intelligent man could fail to recognize that what the socialists, communists and planners were aiming at was the most radical abolition of the individual's freedom and the establishment of government omnipotence. Yet the immense majority of the socialist intellectuals were convinced that in fighting for socialism they were fighting for freedom."[38]

So today's global antitrust crusade isn't the first time freedom was fooled. Nor is it the second. Again, according to Mises, socialists began calling themselves "liberals" (i.e., conservatives in today's language) and professed attachment to a phony "anticommunism" in order to cover over the evident failures and totalitarian abuses of the USSR and its satellites. This disingenuous conservatism opened the way for socialism in the democracies of Europe – and also achieved significant support in the United States.

> "Communism would have today, after the disillusionment brought by the deeds of the Soviets and the lamentable failure of all socialist

---

[38] Ludwig von Mises, *The Anticapitalistic Mentality*, 1972.

experiments, but little chance of succeeding in the West if it were not for this *faked* anticommunism."[39] [Emphasis added.]

Thus we see that antitrust is not only not the first and not the second of the falsehoods promulgated by the deluded or disingenuous defenders of freedom, but merely the latest of the Trojan horses that have unwound promising civilizations. From the birth of freedom in ancient Greece, which Plato waylaid with distortions of key words like "democracy" and "justice,"[40] to the upside-down modern uses of "competition,"[41] "property"[42] and, of course, "liberal,"[43] hopes of freedom have time and again been dashed by despots or their minions twisting words. Those saddened by the loss of their dreams of pursuing happiness no doubt said "it can't happen here" to the very end. They lost their shot in large part because they proved incapable of seeing through the disingenuous linguistic dance of socialism. By the same token, the progress of freedom has resulted only from the success of its defenders at parrying the linguistic tricks and related philosophical traps laid by its enemies.

Today it is primarily antitrust that is playing Alice in Wonderland with the language of freedom. So far, the good intentions of its promoters are in most cases sincere. That is to say, they are in most cases unwitting victims of the general confusion, rather than active promulgators of deliberately misleading propaganda. Therefore, they still by and large deserve a presumption of good intentions. But we must remember that many of those earlier Trojan horses eventually led to despotic abuses that, no matter what you believed about efficiency or fairness or whatever, could not be reconciled with good intentions. While we now assume that those exercising Government power are acting in good faith to serve the public interest by curbing the abuses of self-interested individuals, we will some day soon need to recognize that *self*-interest drives the people of Government, too. In other words, the granting of good intentions should not be automatic, because at some point

---

[39] Ludwig von Mises, *The Anticapitalistic Mentality*, 1972.

[40] Karl R. Popper, *The Open Society and its Enemies:* Vol. 1 – *The Spell of Plato*, 1962.

[41] James V. DeLong, *Antitrust Law For Dummies* – Guest Column, *Tech Central Station*, April 17, 2000. DeLong demonstrates that there are so many potential definitions of "competition" as often to render discussion of it, even in formal regulatory proceedings, confusing at best.

[42] James V. DeLong, *Property Matters*, 1999. DeLong shows the many ways that property today is undermined by Government restrictions on its use.

[43] The devastation wreaked on the cause of freedom by loss of the term "liberal" may be judged by Mises' justification for using it in his 1966 Foreword to the Third Edition of *Human Action*, 1949. "First, I employ the term "liberal" in the sense attached to it everywhere in the nineteenth century and still today in the countries of continental Europe. This usage is imperative because there is simply no other term available to signify the great political and intellectual movement that substituted free enterprise and the market economy for the precapitalistic methods of production; constitutional representative government for the absolutism of kings or oligarchies; and freedom of all individuals for slavery, serfdom and other forms of bondage."

tyranny is tyranny, regardless of the excuse for its adoption. And it is the reflexive granting of good intentions that makes Trojan horses possible.

What's Wrong with Antitrust?

How can such an obscure little law as antitrust cause so much damage?[44] Surely its reputation as a theoretically respectable protector of free markets has *some* foundation, doesn't it? Not in my view. Its errors begin with its first and biggest: antitrust treats monopolies as *bad* things. Wrong. Monopolies are not only the natural and very nearly inevitable result of economic evolution – in spite of Government efforts to block them – but they are the most essential and valuable elements of every economy, particularly a modern one. The more complex an economy becomes, the more its efficient development both promotes and requires monopolization. There is no question, therefore, whether we will have monopolies or not. The only question is whether they will be run by private businesses or by the State.

Although all the antitrust rhetoric vilifying monopolies gives the impression that it is possible to get rid of them, and that it is Government's goal to do so, the first of these is incorrect and the second is a lie. It is neither possible nor desirable to do without monopolies. As mentioned, the only question is whether they will be run by private businesses or by the State. As to Government's goal, while we can't easily attribute disingenuousness to officials (not as long as we're still granting them good intentions, anyway), if Government were a person, say, one named Leviathan, it would be obvious that the claim is a lie. Government has *never* gotten rid of monopolies; it has only transferred control of them from private companies to the State in the devious manner described below. This is not to imply that we should be indifferent about the transfer. Once a private monopoly gets tangled in State tentacles, service suffers, capital deteriorates and corruption rules. To see what we're missing, let's summarize the good things that monopolies can do before the State gets involved.

Individually and collectively, both monopolies themselves – and the process of monopolization pursued simultaneously by many individual monopolists – compel coordination of diverse activities, enabling the economy's various elements to knit together into a unified infrastructure. They enforce compatibility of system and infrastructure components. They efficiently balance the use of resources and

---

[44] The Sherman Act, as quoted in Robert H. Bork's The *Antitrust Paradox – a Policy at War with Itself*: "Section 1. Every contract, combination in the form of trust or otherwise, or conspiracy, in restraint of trade or commerce among the several States, or with foreign nations, is hereby declared illegal . . . Section 2. Every person who shall monopolize, or attempt to monopolize, or combine or conspire with any other person or persons, to monopolize any part of the trade or commerce among the several States, or with foreign nations, shall be guilty of a misdemeanor."

encourage stewardship of scarce ones. They enhance productivity by encouraging coordination, efficient utilization of resources, and innovation. By completing networks, they prevent bottlenecks like those now plaguing the electric power and airline industries. They encourage price stability and non-disruptive turnover of technology platforms. They encourage efficient allocation of capital by sending accurate price signals to all concerned parties. And the combination of all of the above factors encourages more aggressive application of capital to new business formation in the same way that higher stock prices or lower interest rates does. In other words, not only are private monopolies good, but all the supposedly anticompetitive practices that further their development are good, too.

Allowing private monopolization is both consistent with freedom, and creates a kind of property as valid as gold, paper money, credit or corporate stock – and more valuable to capital formation than any of them. Just as a man who owns stock, land or money can parlay his capital through cooperative or competitive arrangements in relation to other owners of such properties, if his assets include monopolies and monopolization opportunities, then he has *supercapital*. Moreover, unlike many modern forms of property, which require elaborate Government sponsored definitions, and defenses of their boundaries mounted by legions of lawyers, monopolies define and defend their own boundaries naturally. They are their own best defense, one that requires no Government definitions, no Government coercion, and no lawyers. And when they are no longer strong enough to defend themselves (or if they don't become strong enough in the first place), that is the natural time for them to turn over the opportunity to others. No need to decide whether seventeen years or twenty years (as with patents) or some other amount of time is appropriate.

Consequently, all those things the Justice Department and other antitrust agencies are suing the monopolists for are the very things we should be applauding them for. From predatory pricing to price-fixing cartels, from tying to gouging to discriminating, from rewarding your friends with favorable deal terms, to refusing to deal with your competitors at all, there is no harm and much benefit to be derived from such activities. All of these so-called anticompetitive practices are no more conflicted and harmful in a free society than the normal self-interested conflicts between buyers and sellers, producers and consumers, wholesale businesses and retail businesses, and the whole host of self-interested actions and maneuverings that drive every thriving economy. Moreover, monopolization – the free application of the monopolist's prerogative over the property he controls – creates the most high-powered form of property and capital in the economy, potentially worth many multiples of the assessable value of the separate assets he owns. The ability to wield them all, to purposefully monopolize, to cut deals and control, is a currency exchangeable in society's most important transactions. And the ability to buy or establish positions of strength through monopolization constitutes both the most valuable property an individual can own, and the most valuable capital a society can boast.

The confusion over the value of monopolies arises primarily because Government-protected monopolies actually *are* bad. Most of the famous monopolies throughout history, of course, either started out bad or became bad when Government got involved. This fact, plus natural jealousy, account for the dismal reputation of monopolies. Antitrust is the modern machine that turns the good monopolies into bad ones. Trustbusters' raison d'être is to put the likes of Standard Oil and Microsoft into the hands of antitrust bureaucrats and the courts. They don't need to nationalize them or break them up to accomplish this. They need only credibly threaten to do so, or subject them to such comprehensive rule making and observation as to circumscribe their monopoly-forming behavior. This effectively puts Government in the position of doling out monopolies through rule making, a modern version of the very process that has earned them a bad name throughout history, such as when kings sold them to their supporters for cash. A sentence and related footnote in Richard Pipes' *Property and Freedom*,[45] for example, reads:

> He [King Charles I] filled his coffers by selling to private interests monopolies (the exclusive right to manufacture and trade in specified commodities). *
>
> *In 1624 the House of Commons had closed this loophole by declaring monopolies illegal. The crown got around this ruling by selling monopolies – renamed "patents" – to persons who invented new and valuable manufacturing processes. Shortly afterward, in 1648, Massachusetts permitted monopoly grants for new inventions "that are profitable for the Countrie." [James W. Ely, Jr., *The Guardian of Every Other Right*, 2nd ed. (New York and Oxford, 1998), 19]. Patents for intellectual property are believed to have originated in fifteenth-century Venice.

Patently Absurd

Do intellectual property rights spur innovation, as advocates claim? I suspect not, at least not compared to the amount of innovation that would exist under a natural property rights regime. Not only would there be more innovation under

---

[45] Richard Pipes, *Property and Freedom*, 1999.

natural property rights, but there would also be a far greater chance that the innovations would be better targeted toward real needs, and a much smaller chance that they would have harmful unintended consequences. While the economic and legal theories underlying the current intellectual property bureaucracies enjoy wide acceptance, even from conservatives, their only real-life effect is to enable a parasitic State to feed off an otherwise healthy society. While the bureaucrats distribute a variety of protected monopoly positions in the form of patents, copyrights, operating licenses and rule sets favoring one company or another, there is little reason to think any of this improves innovation, efficiency or any other public interest. For example, patents probably retard innovation by preventing further invention in and around the general field controlled by the patent.[46] In any case, they distort invention in the direction of a State-devised industrial policy, beefing up boondoggles, and starving useful inventions of the capital going to the boondoggles. The most useful inventions, of course, are those that spring from the creative minds of entrepreneurs and scientists looking to get rich by finding and filling actual human needs. It is a socialist fantasy to imagine that Government help in this process can do anything but retard and distort the result.

Consider the taxpayer-funded fraud known as the biotech business. The field is riddled with phony "nonprofits" getting Government grants to develop drugs on which their for-profit siblings seek patents.[47] The theory behind both the Government (taxpayer) largesse and the patents is that these will enable us to speed up the finding of drugs to cure the world's diseases. Leaving aside the obvious potential for fraud lurking behind such "grantsmanship," and accepting the urgency of the need to improve health, we still must ask one fundamental question. Is this the best way to deploy the social resources available to promote health care innovation represented by such expenditures as the $27 billion NIH budget (2003 projection), or the massive chunks of Medicare and Medicaid going to purchase the patented products created by the NIH effort? The drug companies say patents are

---

[46] On patents, I agree with Rothbard, who would eliminate them. "[W]hile it is true that the *first* discoverer benefits from the [patent],it is also true that his competitors are excluded from production in the area of the patent for many years. And since one patent can build upon a related one in the same field, competitors can often be indefinitely discouraged from *further* research expenditures in the general area covered by the patent. Moreover, the patentee is himself discouraged from engaging in further research in this field, for the privilege permits him to rest on his laurels for the entire period of the patent, with the assurance that no competitor can trespass on his domain. The competitive spur for further research is eliminated." Murray Rothbard, *Man, Economy and State*, 1962. [Emphasis in original.]

[47] "In case after case, scientists closely linked to profit-making companies are applying in the name of nonprofit institutes to obtain multimillion-dollar NIH (National Institutes of Health) grants. In some instances, the same person runs both a nonprofit institute and a for-profit company, and the entities share lab space, equipment and employees. Often, the two entities study the same diseases and drugs, with the nonprofit handling the basic research and the for-profit doing product development." The Wall Street Journal article, *How Adroit Scientists Aid Biotech Companies With Taxpayer Money*, January 30, 2001.

critical to their willingness and ability to fund discoveries.[48] But does it really work that way? Thirty years of the "war on cancer," and $8 billion of NIH funding later, no progress has been made on basic cancer rates. Indeed, it is just possible that the heavy Government involvement is the *reason* we have made so little progress.[49]

There is even mounting evidence that the madcap rush to new drugs may be contributing to some of the problems the patent rush is trying to solve. For example, a significant increase in allergies and asthma in recent years is attributed by some to "immunization" through vaccines.[50] In addition, cystic fibrosis, multiple sclerosis and many other newly burgeoning and unsolved maladies, including many manifestations of cancer, itself, appear to be related to malfunctions of quality control processes that govern cell division and protein expression, especially when these relate to the marshalling of immune responses. Since these are the likely unintended consequences of attacking every disease with a patented drug to boost, supplement or supplant our immune system, it is altogether possible that the patent rush approach to curing disease is what is making us sick. In any case, the medical miracles touted in the drug companies' ads and "breakthrough" research articles are often leavened with the reality of disappointment. Twelve years after the cystic fibrosis gene was discovered with much fanfare, there is still no cure.[51] As for cancer, one promising breakthrough after another has been announced over the years and we don't appear any closer to a cure.[52] The latest "targeted" approach may finally be the answer, but that's what we thought about the rest. In fact, only weeks after the announcement of the "breakthrough" hailed as so exciting that the FDA pulled out all the stops rushing it to approval, it was reported that the targeted cancers were already mutating around the treatment.[53]

Of course scientific exploration always relies on an uncertain combination of skill and luck. So I wouldn't go so far as to imply that no breakthroughs are achievable through the patent approach, or that its elimination would magically

---

[48] The drug companies say it costs them $500 million to develop each new drug. But a "report by Public Citizen puts the amount closer to $100 million." One big reason for the difference: "Taxpayer-funded research also cuts the cost and risk associated with developing new remedies." The Wall Street Journal article, "Drug Industry Exaggerates R&D Costs To Justify Pricing, Consumer Group Says," July 24, 2001.

[49] Except for improvements due to such non-drug-related factors as less smoking and earlier detection, cancer rates have increased 6% since the "war" began. The New Yorker Magazine, *The Thirty Years' War*, Jerome Goopman, June 4, 2001. In his article, Goopman expresses his suspicion that some earlier successes with other diseases were achieved precisely because there was no Government support for them.

[50] The New York Times Sunday Magazine Cover Story, "A Wholesome Poison," June 10, 2001.

[51] Wall Street Journal, front page article, *Cystic Fibrosis Gave Up Its Gene 12 Years Ago; So Where's the Cure? Medical Workers Gain Clues to Workings of Disease, But Most Are Dead Ends*. June 11, 2001.

[52] The New Yorker, *The Thirty Years' War*, Jerome Goopman, June 4, 2001.

[53] "Gleevec, the cancer therapy hailed as a wonder drug against certain types of tumors, turns out to have an Achilles heel after all: More than half of the late-stage patients with chronic myeloid leukemia who initially benefited from the drug have seen their cancer return within six months, an often fatal relapse." Wall Street Journal, "'Wonder Drug' For Leukemia Suffers Setback," June 22, 2001.

double the cure rate. No one can say for sure what the effect of such a switch would be. But it is worth having a fresh look at some of the signs we *can* see in the hopes that they may point to some answers. We can see, for example, that every politician is in favor of some form of free prescription drugs for the elderly. ("Free," of course, means paid for by the taxpayer.) We can see that drug companies are always among the top political contributors. We know that over-prescription of antibiotics has led to so many mutations that we may soon have no effective treatments for some major once curable diseases.[54] We know that prescription drug sales rose 123% in the last five years, that drug ads are taking over our TV screens, and that the elderly – the biggest market for these drugs – may be overmedicated.[55]

Are they overmedicated? Although it seems highly likely to me that they are, I won't argue the point here. I will say, however, that *all* of the financial incentives are pushing in that direction – and point to patents as the source of the problem, if it does exist. In fact, given the pervasive and powerful financial incentives that inevitably flow from the patent approach to innovation, it would be extraordinary if overmedication were *not* the rule, rather than the exception. Of course, overmedication could range from just a little bit too much in the way of unnecessary medication, to the point where the excess is so egregious that medications are, on balance, doing more harm than good. In view of the accelerating speed with which biotech companies are forming around the patent-seeking, Government-funded research devoted to medical intervention, I suspect we are bound to reach that point, if we haven't already. That is, we are bound to reach the point at which our whole modern medical arsenal, with all its wonders, does more harm to its patients than good for them. And, regardless of whether or when we reach that point, the question still remains: Is this the best way to deploy the massive portions of our national income and capital devoted to medical processes? Patents, after all, are promoted as a means of inducing innovation

---

[54] Laurie Garrett, *Betrayal of Trust: The Collapse of Global Public Health*. 2000. Some excerpts from chapter 4 illustrate the now well-known problem: "All evidence indicated that physician's overprescribing antibiotics was driving up drug resistance, but years of successful American Medical Association lobbying had stripped public health authorities of all powers to affect doctors' prescription practices." "When the legal authorities of public health were stripped during the mid-twentieth century, nobody anticipated that hospitals would become centers not only for disease treatment, but also for disease creation." "[Dr. Joshua] Lederberg had won a Nobel Prize for demonstrating how bacteria evolve, eluding antibiotics." "[He now says,] 'We're running out of bullets for dealing with these infections. . . Are we better off today than we were a century ago? In most respects, we're worse off. . . Patients are dying because we no longer have antibiotics that work.' "

[55] Wall Street Journal, "Do No Harm – Doctor Creates a Rift With A Radical Notion: Prescribe Fewer Pills," June 22, 2001. "Dr. [David] Morris blames drug makers for America's ever increasing proclivity for pills. With their legions of sale representatives, sponsorship of the vast majority of research and massive consumer advertising campaigns, the pharmaceuticals industry 'is driving the practice of medicine,' he says." The article says that prescription drug sales grew from $65 billion to $145 billion between 1995 and 2000, that prescriptions filled grew from 2 billion in 1990 to 3 billion in 2000, and that drug makers spent $2.5 billion on advertising in 2000.

through financial incentives. Surely those who make *that* argument would recognize that, if the same system gives financial incentives to overmedicate the elderly, a probable effect will be the overmedication of the elderly. If that system gives incentives for drug companies to buy political influence, drug companies will buy political influence. If it gives incentives for the nation's medical budgets to grow like Topsy, they will grow like Topsy. And if it gives incentives for disease mutations, we will see disease mutations.

And while we're on the topic of incentives, keep in mind the fact that patents achieve their incentive effects because they are monopolies, sole seller privileges granted – in this case – by Government. In other words – and it is worth restating this point for emphasis – it is *Government's deliberate policy to use monopolies as incentives*. Forget for a moment whether those incentives lead to good or bad effects, and just focus on the monopoly incentive itself. Just as Government attempts to incent certain behaviors via monopoly grants, every argument used in justification of that approach would apply as well to the potential opportunity to achieve *private* monopoly positions. That these monopolies are "granted" solely at the discretion of consumers of the monopoly's product, that they are revocable whenever their tastes change, that they cannot be listed in a company's intellectual property portfolio as assets – none of these differences between monopolies won in the market and monopolies granted by Government change the fact that both are very valuable and, therefore, that the incentives provided by both are very powerful. And, while it would be difficult to say which is more valuable, either potentially or empirically, it is obvious from the fact that private monopolies have created quite a few mega-billionaires that the incentives driving private monopolization are extremely powerful, too. In view of these incentives, it is ridiculous to think that the creativity driving the song writer, the scientist or the entrepreneur can only be motivated by the lure of patents and copyrights. There are many places where such creative and inventive talents can give decisive advantages to businesses seeking network monopolies. Therefore, there are many structures one can imagine in which such talents will be rewarded as they aid in the task of improving the services or competitive position of an aspiring network monopolist. While it is impossible to say whether individual inventors or artists would make more or less under a natural approach, it is virtually certain that the amount they make would bear a closer resemblance to the value of their contributions to society.

In contrast, the way it works now is that the antitrust and intellectual property laws work in tandem to empower the governing elite's control of individual initiative. They take away what Government deems to be bad monopolies, like Standard Oil, AT&T and Microsoft, and dole out what Government deems to be good monopolies, like Prozac and one-click shopping.

This undermines potential by, first of all, putting many of the most necessary functions of our infrastructure into the hands of inherently inefficient bureaucracies. The bureaucrats then attempt to manage innovation under *their* auspices by doling out intellectual property.

In consequence, we have a reward system for creativity and invention that is arbitrary at best, because it depends on the arbitrary (or worse) result of influence mongering among politicians, bureaucrats, and privileged companies. The rewards flowing in this system invariably fail to reach large numbers of creators of potentially useful ideas, while bestowing egregiously huge benefits on some of the most laughable charlatans. The patent protected prominence of some drug companies springs to mind, such as those who spend millions singing to us on TV about allergy drugs that don't really do anything,[56] or diet drugs that, unfortunately, do. And what about the music companies whose copyrighted vitriol does such damage to the moral fabric of society? Next time you see one of their gangster "artists" emerging from court on the evening news, consider the fact that the copyright system they defend so strenuously against the likes of Napster doesn't begin to reward artists until they have sold one million CDs. [57] Because the overwhelming majority of artists do not achieve that level of sales, there is nothing in it for the companies to spend much promoting those artists who can't achieve blockbuster status. Who are the potential blockbusters? You're seeing them on the evening news. This is just one example of how a system that creates incentives via grants of Government privilege can produce counterproductive distortions compared to the reputation-based rewards system that would emerge naturally if private monopolists were freely allowed to search out the potential networks.

The Rent Seeker's Ball

In the current environment, it is not surprising that all major U.S. businesses support *both* political parties and their elected officials in rough proportion to their legislative and regulatory clout. Apparently, the political, regulatory and academic cognoscenti, as well as the leaders of the businesses affected by them, all seem willing to accept a little corruption as the price of innovation. They have even invented a term for it – "rent-seeking" – that is at the same time unfathomable to laymen and suggestive of legitimate, if hidden, economic purpose. No sophisticated modern person would suggest that in the real world it could, or even should, be eliminated. And everyone understands with a wink why the biggest political contributions come from the likes of the drug, energy, and airline industries. Meanwhile, it's not a scandal but only news that House Commerce

---

[56] The New York Times Sunday Magazine Cover Story, "The Claritin Effect," March 11, 2001.
[57] The Atlantic Monthly Magazine article, "The Heavenly Jukebox," September, 2000.

Committee Chairman Billy Tauzin "has become the man to see for corporate chieftains in Washington. And a bevy of his friends and former staffers are building careers based on their connections to him."[58]

Does anyone really imagine that consumers will be better off for all this Government involvement? Actually, yes. The bureaucrats, the vast majority of academics, and almost all politicians believe fervently that such Government involvement in property rights as antitrust and patent law is essential to the efficient functioning of capitalism. And so do the businessmen who benefit from the monopolies bestowed by these busybodies. To them, this is the way a capitalist democracy is *supposed* to work. Sure, some of them – the "conservatives" among them – may talk a good free market story. But look closely and you will find that they are actually the ones putting in the last nail. Their arguments about how the lure of owning intellectual property is critical to the willingness of inventors to invent, scientists to inquire, singers to sing, etc., and their blind acceptance of a connection between "competition" and innovation – leaves freedom with no defenders at all. Where'd they go? They have abandoned the field in pursuit of rent. In some instances, the rent-seekers include even those who are most articulate in their denunciations of rent-seeking.

Their actions and in-actions validate the cynical view that sees accommodation to the parasitic tendencies of Government as inevitable, just something we have to do to get our property protected. In this view, neither private markets nor Government are always best at every task. One must look case by case to determine the best mix for any given function, and always recognize that there is bound to be interaction between political and economic processes in any major endeavor. Bureaucrats and rent-seeking, in other words, are just the way it is. This view is often associated with the "Public Choice" school, sometimes called the Virginia school, since one of its founders is Virginia's George Mason University professor James Buchanan, who won the 1986 Nobel Prize in Economics. While the conservative wing of Public Choice sometimes argues that rent-seeking and the self-interest of bureaucrats have so poisoned the application of antitrust that it should be abandoned, they seldom attack the core principles of antitrust, itself. Their failure to do so implies that, for all they know, antitrust's goals may be valid, but merely unattainable in a rent-seeking world. Their calls for abandoning it, therefore, based only on such practical concerns as the lack of empirically demonstrable value, the presence of empirically demonstrable harm, and the probable continuation of both, leave others more optimistic about Government with the impression that these flaws can be cured. Since even the most ardent anti-antitrusters in Public Choice seldom question antitrust either on theoretical or

---

[58] Wall Street Journal, front page article, *Cajun Influence*, May 28, 2001.

violation-of-freedom grounds, the overall effect of their criticism, once again, is to strengthen antitrust by giving the impression that it has been thoroughly vetted by vigorous debate.

Public Choice advocates, especially including conservatives, seem happy enough to join these debates, apparently unaware that such "public" arguments among the academic and political elite over policy are the essence of modern socialism. Consider the following excerpt from an online book about Public Choice:

> Making Assumptions about What People Want
> Like the economists who study the market economy, Public Choice theorists examine democratic political structures in terms of how well we can expect them to give the people what they really want. We might say that the ultimate objective of Public Choice is to help people get more of what we think they want. To achieve this objective, we must make assumptions about the things that people want. We then ask about the conditions under which various democratic rules and institutions are likely to help them satisfy the assumed wants. If our assumptions about wants are correct, our analyses will be *relevant*. Otherwise, they will not be relevant. In either case, the Public Choice scholar states his assumptions for all to see and to possibly dispute.[59]

With such a mission in mind, the policy-making elite must view freedom as only a *potential* means to a social welfare end, *expendable* if results don't measure up. And with such a mission in mind, theory is just a tool to approximate what might be worth testing, first in the lab, then on the public. According to this modus operandi, public debate – not private creativity, competition and natural selection – is the best path to innovation and efficient institutions.

I first came across this nonsensical notion when I participated in the SEC's "comment period" process. As I learned to my dismay, not only does this process destroy innovation, but it also produces lousy institutions. Comment periods and other forms of public debate are only the most visible part of the rent-seeking frenzy by which Government processes extinguish freedom. But, irony of ironies, everyone involved, including all of Wall Street's presumed conservatives, participated fully in this process with nary a peep about its socialist character. At regulatory conferences you could almost hear them calling each other "comrade" as they praised themselves and each other for joining the debates and exhorted

---

[59] J. Patrick Gunning, *Understanding Democracy – An Introduction to Public Choice*, 2001.

others to do so, too. The haughty presumption that they were entitled to deference for their good intentions merely because they aired their opinions in public debate was breathtaking. Numerous times I heard senior officials at important financial institutions like large mutual funds berate any who failed to participate with implied threats like "If you don't make yourselves heard, you'll get what you deserve." And I never heard any hint of skepticism that the coercive measures that would spring from these debates would lack legitimacy due to the obviously socialist character of the process.

It is another fine irony that Public Choice, a school that contains some of the most hard-nosed critics of Government's failures due to rent-seeking, pushes a process that is tailor made both for neutralizing their own criticisms and for expanding and perpetuating rent-seeking. But there is a Catch-22 in their prescriptions: imposing on people "what we think they want" can never be compatible with individual dignity and freedom and, therefore – assuming that people do want freedom – will always fail on its own terms. The fact that Public Choice recognizes the self-interest of bureaucrats and tries, with this in mind, to devise institutions that give us what we want in spite of these limitations is distressing. It is no different in terms of freedom than the old Marxist slogan "to each according to his needs." In fact, it's worse. Because it realistically includes acknowledgement of the flaws in Government processes, it is much harder to dismiss as ineffective in giving us what we want. Think of it as a modern form of the "voluntary" slavery of feudal times in which villeins or serfs "accepted" bondage in return for being taken care of.

The Public Choice view is also consistent with that which sees bureaucrats as an extension of those processes in primitive slave cultures by which the powerful forced the weak to produce food and other benefits for them. And it is consistent with the views of those cultural evolutionists who cite the habit of early civilizations to both enslave conquered peoples and to allow only as much freedom or consumption for their own people as was consistent with the exercise and maintenance of their leaders' power. Jared Diamond, for example, sees the appearance of ancient "bureaucrats" as one sign that a civilization has reached a significant level of development.[60] And William McNeil describes the powerful roles played in human social evolution by the parasite twins: "micro-parasites," such as germs and blood-sucking bugs, and "macro-parasites," such as ruling classes that enslave or control others with their armies and Governments.[61] Given the rent-seeking machinations of today's bureaucrats, lawyers, politicians and businessmen, it is anything but inconsistent to view our own process as an example of what these brutally realistic observers have described.

---

[60] Jared Diamond, *Guns, Germs and Steel: The Fates of Human Societies,* 1999.
[61] William McNeill, *Plagues and Peoples,* 1977.

The Spirit of 'Seventy-Six

Realistic and historically accurate as these views may be, the American experiment in individual freedom and limited Government was meant to be a step beyond such methods. Unless our Founders had in mind an elaborate deception by which we would more readily accept tyranny if we could be fooled into believing it was freedom,[62] we really did and do believe in every individual's right to be protected by law against the arbitrary exercise of Government power. To this end, the most important right, in a practical sense, is the right to property. The question, however, is how do we define "property"? And, more important, *who* defines it? Is the concept of property essentially innate, inhering in the individual's actions and natural relationships with his surroundings and other people in a way that can be universally recognized? Or is it something that Government must define? I believe and hope it is the former, and have come across several libertarian articulations of natural property rights that work for me. Murray Rothbard, for example, says individuals should be able to do whatever does not physically harm anyone else, or threaten to do so.[63] Such naturally free individuals can do what they will to better their condition and may thereby accumulate their own property as a result of whatever commercial arrangements and contracts they can devise. Property originally comes into existence in the following way: Starting with the paradigmatic example of land, a person can occupy land that is not owned or occupied by anyone else and establish his right to it as property through the sweat of his brow, such as by building a house or tilling the soil. Thereafter it becomes *his* property to use, not use, or sell to someone else. No person or Government may take such property away from the rightful owner, or use it without his permission. The authority to apply coercion to enforce such rights, like the rights themselves, would derive from universally recognizable common law principles, and could be exercised by private enforcement agencies (in Rothbard's vision) or by a Government that is constitutionally bound to respect those common law provisions (in my vision).

Conventional conservative wisdom, in contrast, holds that property rights come from the State. In this view, without giving the State authority to define, articulate and enforce property rights, they would not exist, and man's progress to date would turn to sand. Government not only has the right to define and enforce

---

[62] This may sound absurd, but, according to Karl R. Popper, Plato, for one, and Marx, for another, did advocate just such deceptions. *The Open Society and Its Enemies:* Vol. 1 – *The Spell of Plato*, 1962. Also see Francis Jennings, *The Creation of America*, 2001, which, according to its cover, "reveals as war propaganda the revolutionary rhetoric about liberty and virtue."

[63] Murray Rothbard, *The Ethics of Liberty,* 1982.

property rights, in this view Government implicitly owns all property or potential property until it is moved by grant, license, auction or otherwise into private hands. Rothbard's squatters would not be able to establish ownership by his first-productive-use principle, but would have to somehow get it from Government.

Comparing first-use squatting versus Government-directed distribution as means of originating property and moving it to private hands, few people today would think of the former as legitimate, while most would assume that the latter is just the way the world works. We don't, after all, have much recent experience of either method when it comes to originating property in land, which still provides the prime example for most people of the concept of property. But Rothbard's squatting is not the occupy-to-steal strategy you read about in which indigents might claim a right to someone else's property because they moved in while he was away. Rothbard would call that theft. Perhaps to get past the assumption that squatting is less than legitimate, Rothbard, like Mises, gives examples of Robinson Crusoe to establish that there was a time when land was so abundant that no one cared to own it.[64] While I found his examples convincing, others may consider them unrealistic or irrelevant to current property rights theory. But there is today a massive example of the squatting principle in action, namely, monopolization. All monopoly formation involves the creation of products, services, processes, alliances or other network formation activities that constitute new, first use property – or would, if Government took a natural law approach to monopolization activities. The sole seller position established through monopolization would create property in the unique connections, pathways or markets that did not exist before, or at least did not exist in exactly the way that the monopolist has created.

Obviously, Government does not recognize monopolization as a valid technique to establish property rights to a monopoly or anything else, even less so than it would recognize property in land to someone who began farming or mining on a Government plot. One way to understand Government's antipathy to private monopoly is to recognize the threat it presents to the Government prerogative over property. And one way to see why we would be better off if Government did not have a property prerogative is to see how it has always screwed up the role. From the distribution of land in the American West in the 19th century, which was never successful and is now being reversed,[65] to the distribution of spectrum via flubbed

---

[64] And Carl Menger, the founder of the Austrian School, is credited with developing the idea that property begins with scarcity. Later "Austrians" extended the concept to note that the more dense and complex an economy becomes, the more important the development of property rights to allocate the scarcities thereby generated. Carl Menger, *Principles of Economics*, 1871, and particularly the introduction to the 1976 English translation by Friedrich A. Hayek.

[65] The New York Times op-ed by Richard Manning, "Destiny Revisits the Great Plains," July 10, 2001.

auctions today,[66] there is no evidence that Government can handle a property role effectively. Yet even as the role expands from physical property to intangible property, we rely more than ever on Government to define and enforce property rights. And conservatives are often at the forefront of those justifying this role.[67]

One thing I'll grant: If Government is doing the defining, then it may be that Government also has to do the enforcing. But three problems will gather increasing force if we continue to do it this way: 1) the amount of potential property will be less, 2) the proportion of it that can be protected will be less, and 3) Government will increasingly be seen as a wedge between our actual and potential property, which will lead to massive dissatisfaction and potentially revolution. Under a Government definition regime, the natural desire of the governing elite for greater control will move definitions toward those which require ever greater coercion to enforce. In contrast, natural definitions would allow the creation of far more proprietary capital, such as the ideas behind both the network monopolies and the intellectual property of the Information Age. Indeed, whole new categories of property would emerge as more complex social and economic systems evolve. The longer the Government definition regime is retained, the more acute the conflict between these two potential methods will become. Eventually, enforcing Government-defined property claims will become nearly impossible, even with intolerable coercion. And the gap between our potential and our reality, both

---

[66] New York Times article, "Against All Odds, A Telecom Rebirth," July 15, 2001. The article describes the NextWave debacle, which, in addition to the problems described, is headed toward costing the taxpayer $14 billion: "And despite bitter differences, *all sides agree that the main victims have been consumers.* Clamoring for better cell phone service as the airwaves have become more crowded, they increasingly find calls dropped or not completed, a problem that could have been greatly alleviated years ago had the licenses at stake here been put to use by now." And "The company [NextWave] has become the nation's largest corporate political donor in recent years, and its lobbying operations are headed by James Cicconi, a former top aide to the first President Bush. It employs a huge group of inside lobbyists, outside lobbying firms and lawyers. Others opposing NextWave, like Verizon, Cingular, VoiceStream and Nextel Communications, have soaked up much of the remaining legal and lobbying talent in Washington. Industry lobbyists include a firm run by Anthony Podesta, brother of John D. Podesta, the former chief of staff for Mr. Clinton, and the firm formerly headed by Nicholas E. Calio, President Bush's top assistant for legislative affairs. A large number of former government officials now work for NextWave's competitors. NextWave and its allies also flexed political muscle. Their team includes Haley Barbour, a former chairman of the Republican National Committee, and Robert L. Livingston, the Congressman who was elected House speaker but resigned before taking the post when it was revealed that he had had an extramarital affair. The company and its allies, prodigious political fund-raisers, persuaded two Democratic Senators, Robert G. Torricelli of New Jersey and Charles E. Schumer of New York, to join three House members in filing a brief in the Washington appeal supporting the company." [Emphasis added.]

[67] "The technological turmoil we are now undergoing is requiring us to rethink and refine concepts of intellectual property rights. Obviously, government must be heavily involved in this process. No matter what view one takes about the derivation of property rights, even if one believes that they are a product of natural law and not within the power of governments to withhold, governments must always define them at the margins and enforce them. This is especially true for intellectual property, which is more dependent on government than physical assets. Land or machinery exists independently, whatever a government says, and can be protected by fences and force, but a patent or copyright exists only within the context of a system of law." James V. DeLong, "Intellectual Property and Antitrust Enforcement"; House Oversight Hearing on the Antitrust Enforcement Agencies, April 12, 2000.

individually and as a nation, will become ever more palpable. The combination of these two factors – intolerable coercion and a sense of shortfall relative to potential – will, unless reversed, lead to an illegitimacy crisis for our Government.

England, where the property rights we have now were largely developed, faced such illegitimacy crises repeatedly during the last millennium, often resolving them in the direction of natural definitions. In fact, the very concept of property, from its origins in ancient Greece on down, emerged only as individuals wrested control of the definition of property from kings and the State. Only by establishing the right to control definitions through such common law milestones as Magna Carta[68] were we freed of the arbitrary power of the State. There was much backsliding, though, as the crown sought to exploit definitional loopholes and worm its way back into exercising arbitrary control over property.[69] And by no means were definitional conflicts always resolved in favor of individual rights. Quite the contrary, especially in Russia, which was 600 years or so behind England in their development.[70] This was not surprising, coming as they did from a tradition in which the czar technically owned not only all the land, but also owned his people and their personal items.

But give rent-seeking its due. Freedom got under way only when the top nobles wanted to take advantage of a weak king (or such exigencies as his need for money to wage war) to win special rights for themselves. The nobles in no way intended to extend rights down to the lower classes, much less to slaves, villeins or serfs – indeed their rent-seeking coalitions would certainly have collapsed at the very mention of such democratic heresies. But, though the original nobles sought only their own property, later on the same logic by which they got theirs would

---

[68] Article 61 of the Magna Carta (1215) moved significantly toward giving definitional power to the people, when it gave power to determine satisfaction in disputes with the Crown to the barons: "[I]f we, or our justice, or our bailiffs, or any one of our servants shall have transgressed against any one in any respect, or shall have broken one of the articles of peace or security, and our transgression shall have been shown to four barons of the aforesaid twenty five: those four barons shall come to us, or, if we are abroad, to our justice, showing to us our error; and they shall ask us to cause that error to be amended without delay. And if we do not amend that error, or, we being abroad, if our justice do not amend it within a term of forty days from the time when it was shown to us or, we being abroad, to our justice: the aforesaid four barons shall refer the matter to the remainder of the twenty five barons, and those twenty five barons, with the whole land in common, shall distrain and oppress us in every way in their power,-- namely, by taking our castles, lands and possessions, and in every other way that they can, until amends shall have been made *according to their judgement*." [Emphasis added.]

[69] For example, the step forward for freedom referred to in the previous footnote was soon reversed: "The famous clause, probably the contribution of Stephen Langton, then Archbishop of Canterbury, was subject to continuous attack by defenders of the royal prerogatives, and was omitted from later versions of the charter when the king regained power." William A. Niskanen, Cato's Letter #14, "On the Constitution of a Compound Republic," The Cato Institute, 2001.

[70] Richard Pipes, *Property and Freedom*, 1999.

inevitably be read to include all those lower classes they originally meant to exclude.[71]

Hanging onto our gains hasn't been made any easier by philosophers like Thomas Hobbes who argued that whatever rights we had wrested from the State wouldn't be enforceable without the State's coercive powers. And the legitimizer of Leviathan has many descendents among today's conservatives. The good news is that there is now virtual unanimity among philosophers and most governments that *everyone* should be able own property. The bad news is that, with all groups now entitled to it, rent-seeking has shifted to defining what property is, and everybody wants to get into the act. So Leviathan is back in business, mediating the conflicts between group interests as property definitions change. This, of course, is exactly what they should not do in a society that respects the Rule of Law, which – if it means anything – means that the rules should be the same for all, and very nearly for all time.[72] But today's rules regarding property are very different for different groups of people as a result of rent-seeking, and they are constantly in flux as society moves beyond land, physical objects and financial assets to the intellectual property of the Information Age.

Just a few examples: How do we decide whether "scientists" should be allowed to "discuss" (exchange papers about) encryption technologies, knowledge of which could be used to circumvent copyrights of recorded songs. How about "non-scientists"? Does the First Amendment protect coded "songs" or "poems" whose intent is to spread computer instructions to hack the encryption protection of copyrighted songs or movies? How do we enforce copyrights to songs that are "shared" on Napster by teenagers who clearly have not taken seriously their parents' admonitions to respect the property of others? (These kids respond

---

[71] Even in Russia, soon after Catherine the Great's *Noble Charter* in 1785, Catherine and others were listening to the property-based economic theories of the Physiocrats, which had obvious potential beyond the upper classes. "Although Catherine applied the teachings of the Physiocrats only to the upper class, it did not escape her, and some of her more thoughtful contemporaries, that they were germane to peasants as well. From the middle of the eighteenth century voices were heard arguing that peasants would be more productive and tranquil if given freedom along with title to the land they cultivated. An international contest launched in 1766 by the St. Petersburg Free Economic Society on her initiative for the best response to the question whether the peasant should own land which he cultivated awarded the first prize to a Frenchman, Bearde de l'Abbaye, who answered affirmatively on the grounds that one hundred peasant-proprietors would outproduce two thousand serfs." Richard Pipes, *Property and Freedom*, 1999.

[72] Friedrich Hayek and Bruno Leoni make the best arguments in this direction I have found. Leoni, in *Freedom and The Law* (1961), for example, says that in order for all new interpretations of law to be accepted universally by everyone, they must, from everyone's perspective, prevent every person from doing anything that he would not want someone else to do to him. This "negative" Golden Rule allows for only a very slow evolution of law, because all laws must by common agreement be universally applicable to everyone, and always applied. This is what is meant by the Rule of Law, which evolves according to a common law process of passing every potential new interpretation by these principles, and results in universally accepted and acknowledged law. Both Hayek and Leoni warn, quixotically it seems, of the power of "legislation" to avoid this process and produce illegitimate laws that are not only not universally accepted, but are in the end not even accepted by a majority of the people to whom they apply.

without compunction (What-a-ya-gonna-do?) to ads from multibillion-dollar computer companies (Apple) to "rip, mix, burn." Do they think their parents don't know that "rip" means "steal"?) What do we do about it if all these kids can evade attempts by Napster to comply with a judge's ban on their swapping practices by inventing word twists that hide the actual titles they are swapping? What if they use decentralized swapping methods that, unlike Napster, can't be shut down anyway? How do we decide how long patents should last on AIDS drugs, as opposed to, say, arthritis drugs, or allergy drugs, or one-click shopping methods for the Internet? How do we decide under what conditions compulsory licensing of patented drugs in foreign countries with rampant health problems is appropriate? Would compulsory licensing ever be appropriate for one-click shopping? If it works for drugs, why not? If we decide it isn't appropriate, either in some cases, or at all, what if we can't stop it? Should it matter if the patients most in need of the latest medicines are old? Or poor? Does it matter? How do we determine whether a copyright that now protects the descendents of Margaret Mitchell are violated by a modern parody of *Gone With the Wind* which makes liberal use of the original's text to imply criticism of Mitchell's attitude about blacks. Should the race of either author matter? Does it?

It should be clear to even the most casual observer that "property" is bound to become arbitrary, conditional, and ultimately meaningless as a defense of individual freedom under these circumstances. Number one, technology and globalization are making it easier and easier to evade our State-enforced protections. Number two, with the allocation of property obviously the result of effectively arbitrary decisions, then we *must* blame the State for any unfair results of that allocation, and we *must* permit petitions for redress of any *alleged* unfairness. This gives "inequality" a voice. Thus, inequalities – real or imagined – both within rich nations like ours, and between ours and Third World countries, force us to justify the application of our principles regarding property in the face of their increasingly untenable allocation consequences. Those consequences range from the seemingly trivial denial of our children's "right" to free music to the denial of health care "rights" to disease sufferers around the world. Conservative hard-liners scoff at such concerns and insist on tougher sanctions for infringement. But that just won't work. Once the allocation of property is obviously based on arbitrary decisions, it is impossible to maintain the moral authority to enforce property rights with any legitimacy. And once that happens, the coercion applied to enforce them anyway comes more and more to resemble the raw power of a police state.

The seemingly trivial infringements of our children are not nearly as harmless as they might seem. In fact, their attitudes are already shared by large swaths of the digital elite. And the fact that the fastest growing website to date is a non-public company based on piracy gives little hope that moral suasion can put the genie back in the bottle. The more enduring lesson is likely to be that issues like this are decided not on principle but on the basis of who has Leviathan's ear. The notion that your property is yours, that you can deny its use to others or the State, has become a quaint concept that our youth will only learn about in history books (and probably not there either, because Leviathan writes them). As in czarist Russia, increasingly in today's America, you keep your property only at the pleasure of the State.

In fact, the great American road to riches itself now entails submitting to all manner of processes prescribed by the State. The more Leviathan gets to define our opportunities, to box in our actions and monitor our movements, the more dependent on him we become for the opportunities we have, and the more conditional on his good graces our "property" becomes. Trade secrets based on original inventions must be filed with the patent office for all to see (assuming we want to realize any property value from them). Contracts, discussions and e-mail are potential evidence of wrongful conduct, and Leviathan retains the right to subpoena them. Businessmen are wary of talking about the most fundamental aspects of their businesses, like price, because their employees, lawyers, competitors or others may rat on them for price fixing to get amnesty for themselves.[73] Even the richest and seemingly most powerful are back to begging for bread, seeking Leviathan's favor by filing forms, participating in public debates, and informing on competitors.

Thus, Scott McNealy, CEO of Sun Microsystems, and an avowed libertarian, lectures reporters on "economics 101," by which he means antitrust theory, while begging for some of Microsoft's market. Why? Because, as Leviathan whispers in his ear, "Bill Gates has been harming competitors – like Sun Microsystems, don't you see?" And, dutiful servant that he is, McNealy rallies groups of Bill Gates wannabes and Microsoft competitors, like Oracle's CEO Larry Ellison. And the crowd pleases Leviathan greatly by demanding that the Royal Guards tie up Microsoft like Gulliver in Lilliput. Ellison even sends investigators to comb through Microsoft's trash looking for material with which to inform on his competitor. A truly libertarian approach, such as Rothbard's, that would only bar *physical* harm, is lost on McNealy and Ellison. While the Rothbard

---

[73] The New York Times article, *The World Gets Tough on Price Fixing*, June 3, 2001. "The new policy made amnesty automatic if the company came in before an investigation began and permitted broad amnesty afterward to the first company to offer assistance. It also covered all executives from that company who cooperated, a significant inducement because violations of the Sherman Act carry a potential prison sentence of three years for every count, in addition to virtually limitless fines. 'The amnesty program is the [antitrust] division's most effective generator of large cases, and it is the [Justice] department's most successful leniency program,' said James M. Griffin, a deputy assistant attorney general in the antitrust division who heads its criminal enforcement office and plays the pivotal role of deciding which cases will be filed. 'The program is unique,' he said. 'No other U.S. voluntary disclosure program offers as great an opportunity or incentive for companies to self-report and cooperate.'"

approach would allow for a natural route to a universally accepted definition of property, the McNealy "libertarianism" involves heavy Government interpretation, definition, and coercion – not to mention informing on your fellow businessmen – which inevitably leads to arbitrariness. But which view did our Founders favor?

The Framers of our Constitution were anything but clear on the matter, in spite of a Herculean and courageous effort to be clear. The famous words in the Declaration of Independence laid out the principles: we have "unalienable Rights . . . [to] Life, Liberty, and the Pursuit of Happiness." Did they choose the "Pursuit of Happiness" formulation, instead of the more common "life, liberty and property" phrase or John Locke's original "life, liberty and estates" because they were unsure that property or estates belonged in that hallowed pantheon of unalienable rights? Or was the change due to a more general or even prophetic understanding that the word "property" did not convey enough protection for freedom? In any case, Adam Smith, who published The Wealth of Nations in the same year (1776), writes eloquently on how a man's capital derives from his own labor, deployed however he wishes, provided his actions do not injure anyone else.[74] Smith also tied the accumulation of property and capital to the Government-protected right of the individual to pursue his own interest.[75] Obviously, Smith and Rothbard are pretty much in synch on the matter.

Unfortunately, in spite of the Framers' heroic efforts, their Declaration and Constitution did not prevent modern America from adopting the McNealy/Ellison interpretation. For all we know, at least some of them may even have intended that interpretation in the next line: "That to secure these Rights, Governments are instituted among men, deriving their just Powers from the Consent of the Governed." In any case, it is increasingly difficult today for individuals to know what their property rights are, and Government is increasingly involved at every turn in defining them, and redefining them, and redefining them, and redefining them. In this environment, not only are many forms of intangible property, such as

---

[74] "The property which every man has in his own labour, as it is the original foundation of all other property, so it is the most sacred and inviolable. The patrimony of a poor man lies in the strength and dexterity of his hands; and to hinder him from employing this strength and dexterity of his hands; and to hinder him from employing this strength and dexterity in what manner he thinks proper without injury to his neighbor is a plain violation of this most sacred property. It is a manifest encroachment upon the just liberty both of the workman and of those who might be disposed to employ him. As it hinders the one from working at what he thinks proper, so it hinders the others from employing whom they think proper. To judge whether he is fit to be employed may surely be trusted to the discretion of the employers whose interest it so much concerns. The affected anxiety of the law-giver lest they should employ an improper person is evidently as impertinent as it is oppressive." Adam Smith, *The Wealth of Nations*, 1776.

[75] "[T]his capital has been silently and gradually accumulated by the private frugality and good conduct of individuals, by their universal, continual, and uninterrupted effort to better their own condition. It is this effort, protected by law and allowed by liberty to exert itself in the manner that is most advantageous, which has maintained the progress of England towards opulence and improvement in almost all former times, and which, it is to be hoped, will do so in all future times." Adam Smith, *The Wealth of Nations*, 1776.

intellectual property, coming undone, but so is physical property, such as land.[76] This is clearly *not* what the Framers had in mind. Nonetheless, it is not only what the likes of McNealy and Ellison vociferously espouse, but it is also the evident philosophy of their antagonists, such as Bill Gates. In the antitrust duels, it is difficult to tell which side is doing more damage to freedom: those who challenge monopolists, or the monopolists and their conservative seconds. I believe it is the latter.

Bill Gates Is a Socialist

The most effective legitimizers of antitrust are businesses. This seems ironic, since they and their hired guns always seem to be involved in bitter arguments with bureaucrats. But the fact is that all of them are, or hope to be, successful at the rent-seeking game. And questioning the legitimacy of rent-seeking is, to say the least, not good rent-seeking strategy. So the public sees a highly contentious, adversarial process, laden with hyperbole delivered by the best lawyers, lobbyists and PR firms, not to mention occasional cameo appearances by the nation's wealthiest businessmen and its most prominent elected officials.[77] Nonetheless, the ongoing act of engagement in this battle constitutes the most compelling endorsement possible of the competition theories that give rise to it. In spite of appearances, there is no philosophical disagreement about the legitimacy and basic purpose of antitrust, regardless of the vehemence of arguments over fine points or the outcome of any particular cases. That is because the arguments are almost always *only* over details, technicalities, interpretations, precedents and other legal

---

[76] James V. DeLong, *Property Matters*, 1999, and Richard Pipes, *Property and Freedom*, 1999.

[77] The New York Times article, "Microsoft Case Back in Play, And the Lobbying Heats Up," June 30, 2001. In a vivid display of modern rent-seeking, the article says: "Microsoft has catapulted its political activities from a tiny Washington operation to one of the most formidable lobbying and legal powerhouses in town. In the last two-year election cycle, the company and its employees were the fifth-largest political donors in the nation, giving some $4.66 million, according to the Center for Responsive Politics, and another $12 million to lobbyists. By contrast, when the case began seven years ago, the company and its senior executives had given a total of $10,000 to the two political parties and $33,000 to federal candidates and had one lobbyist on the company payroll. Microsoft and its allies have hired a virtual dream team of lobbyists. They have included Haley Barbour, the former chairman of the Republican National Committee; Tom Downey, the former Democratic congressman from Long Island; Vin Webber, the former Republican congressman from Minnesota; Jack Quinn, the former White House counsel; Slade Gorton, the former senator from Washington; C. Boyden Gray, the White House counsel to former President George Bush and his law partner, Lloyd N. Cutler, a counsel to former Presidents Jimmy Carter and Clinton; and Ralph Reed, the former executive director of the Christian Coalition and an adviser to President Bush. On the other side, AOL Time Warner (which owns Netscape, the rival browser to Microsoft's Internet Explorer, and offers a number of other competing products and services) and its allies have spent comparable amounts and retained a list of luminaries. In the appeals case alone, the opponents of Microsoft retained three former United States solicitors general of widely different ideological stripes — Walter E. Dellinger III, Robert H. Bork and Kenneth W. Starr — and their large law firms to put pressure on the government to continue the lawsuit. In the last election cycle, AOL and its executives contributed nearly $2 million to federal campaigns and millions more in lobbying. Other Microsoft competitors have contributed nearly as much in political donations, evening the political matchup."

minutiae. Why? Because it is these minutiae that determine success or failure for the client businesses, first in the legal/regulatory sphere, and then – for those who have won a rent-seeking advantage – in the "marketplace." Such arguments over antitrust details can have no other effect than to validate its basic principles, ever more firmly establishing Government's reign over the innovation process. That conservatives cannot drop out of the courtroom long enough to point this out is why freedom has so little chance anymore. *Everyone* has been co-opted.

From Bill Gates on down, every argument proffered in defense of Microsoft in its ongoing antitrust trials is to the effect that the company is not a monopoly and never attempted to become one. Not only its own attorneys, but legions of supposedly conservative academics from right wing think tanks, "independent" institutes and elsewhere who came out to defend this most visible symbol of capitalism, all of them, without exception, agreed essentially with Gates. No one argued that it's their right to be a monopoly if they want to. No one said that – provided they didn't physically harm or threaten to physically harm anyone – they were fully within their rights as free Americans to engage in any monopolization or anticompetitive tactics of their choosing. They didn't argue their right to do these things, because even the slightest hint that they were aware that they might have knowingly engaged in them would imply antitrust guilt – and the loss of billions. So instead they made fools of themselves trying to prove they didn't do what all of America knew they were doing.

Of course being willing to make a fool of oneself is par for the course in a rent-seeking world; with so much money at stake it is far from a bad legal strategy to adopt the assumptions of the judge, no matter what you think. So neither side would dream of basing its case on the illegitimacy of antitrust. With that question off the table, the arguments in court all boil down to: *You Are a Monopoly. Am Not a Monopoly. Are. Am not. Are. Not. Are. Not.* Of course, being a monopoly is not in itself illegal. Plaintiffs then have to prove monopolization. But this, too, boils down to: *Did. Didn't. Did. Didn't.* There are no bright lines here, which is why antitrust is such a great gig for lawyers and academics squaring off against each other. Liberals generally attack all monopolies, while conservatives try to get them off the hook. But that doesn't matter. It doesn't matter who takes what sides in these debates. Nor does it matter who is correct as a matter of law, or who wins. What matters is that the very existence of the arguments only solidifies the impression that antitrust is valid, if properly applied. Since the losing side at least will always argue that any particular application could be improved upon, the theoretical dream of proper application will always remain. So *everyone* continues to agree on the theoretical validity of antitrust. *Everyone* can believe that, if only the other side would drop their stupid arguments – or be overruled by a wiser court – perfect application would result.

Both sides always agree, in other words, that deliberately pursuing monopoly is evil. The plaintiff argues that the defendant pursued monopoly; the defendant denies it. Both have adopted the right strategy, because the alternative (questioning the legitimacy of antitrust) has zero probability of success, while the standard approach almost always has a roughly even chance of winning the case, and a nearly certain chance of improving the career prospects of those arguing it. The case has a 50/50 chance of success, because, given the arbitrariness of antitrust application, there are always thousands of people who will agree that the accused is guilty, and there are always thousands of people who will agree that the accused is innocent. With nothing but shifting political winds to ultimately decide after all the appeals are exhausted, whether the accused is guilty or innocent, even the most expert have little better than a 50/50 chance of guessing the outcome. And those totally ignorant of the law or the issues don't have much worse of a chance; such is the gaming potential of arbitrary justice.

The most visible evidence that this arbitrariness is the reality in antitrust prosecutions is the spinmeisters trying to sway public opinion on the courthouse steps before and after all trial sessions and related events. If the law were clear – that is, if the Rule of Law governed antitrust matters – this would not be so. The law would determine the outcome, not public opinion. You would not be guilty if Democrats are in power, but innocent if Republicans are in office; guilty if the public mood is to soak the rich, but innocent if the mood favors stock market wealth. If the Rule of Law governed, you would not see so many reversals on appeal, nor would you see expectations of a Microsoft breakup change radically as the White House changes hands. You would not see different courts reaching radically different conclusions on such matters as what market shares constitute monopoly power, on whether Herfindahl indexes (a statistical measure of market concentration) should be used in the determination, or on whether a 10-year versus a 5-year lease for shoe manufacturing equipment is allowable. That such arbitrariness has always been the reality in antitrust cases proves beyond question that antitrust is inconsistent with the very concept of property, which from the beginning has meant ownership not subject to the arbitrary whims of the crown or State. That billions regularly change hands based only on the shifting fancies of a policy that, in Robert Bork's phrase, is "at war with itself" is, at best, amusing. As to why the careers of those arguing the cases are almost certainly enhanced by accepting antitrust? What else can they do? *Unless* they accept it, they have no careers. *If* they accept it, they have a reasonable chance of winning half the time, whether they are any good or not. And every case they argue further establishes their credibility to argue one side or the other of future cases.

But, however good the universality of the denial defense is for attorneys' careers, win or lose it has the effect of preventing any future claim that it is your right to do what you are denying you did. Moreover, no one else can either. In a typical case, plaintiffs (usually some combination of competitors, ambitious bureaucrats and lawyers) will accuse a monopolist of, say, "predatory pricing." The monopolist will deny he did any such thing, hoping there are no smoking guns in his e-mails, and marshal academic expert witnesses to demonstrate the great difficulty of making the tactic work, anyway. Regardless of whether the academic arguments make economic or legal sense, and regardless of whether they do or do not sway the court or the public, the one thing proved beyond any doubt is this: If the accused monopolist *did* engage in predatory pricing, he *would be* guilty. Therefore, neither he nor anyone else better try it. Of course, in practice, they do try it again, in fact over and over. But they become more sophisticated at figuring out which kinds of predation are less likely to be detected by the gendarmes, and they become ever more creative at the fine art of disingenuous denial. The situation rewards those who can engage in predation without getting caught, the crafty, the liars. It also rewards those whose antitrust teams and legal lobbying crew can trip up the less sophisticated liars among their competitors. The situation hinders those who would more simply turn their creative energies toward the honest task of competing hard for the consumer's dollar by fashioning whatever business arrangements would serve that end.

This scenario is repeated ad infinitum across all the categories and nuances of potentially anticompetitive behavior. Not only is predatory pricing blocked, but so are many kinds of discrimination that are deemed predatory (or anticompetitive, or monopolistic – the categories tend to blend), such as getting your customers or suppliers to not deal with your competitors as a condition of buying from or selling to you. Similarly, market division (I won't invade your turf, if you don't invade mine), collusion with competitors for almost any purpose (such as fixing prices or boycotting new technologies), and deliberately attempting to get, protect or extend a monopoly by any of the above or other means are prohibited. And many more esoteric offenses, such as various forms of "tying" or "bundling," are frequently off limits, too, sometimes per se, and sometimes only if they can be shown to be harmfully anticompetitive under a "rule of reason." That determination as well as the final outcome at trial will often depend on whether the court accepts the defendant's terminology or the plaintiff's. Rather than "tying" or "bundling," for example, Microsoft likes to speak of "integration," which has a nice politically correct sound to it. Its opponents, in contrast, are now calling it "bolting," which rhymes nicely with "revolting."[78]

---

[78] Robert H. Bork and Kenneth W. Starr, "Court Ruling Was No Victory For Microsoft," Wall Street Journal op-ed, July 5, 2000. The authors, often hailed as leading lights of the conservative movement, try to spin the issue against Microsoft with statements like "Microsoft's bolting of its operating system and browser into a single package was an illegal tying arrangement." Several weeks later in a New York Times article (July 19, 2001, "Microsoft Asks for

This call is particularly hard to make, because – integrated or bolted – the end product is both incredibly attractive to many consumers and incredibly useful for anyone who wants to get, protect or extend a monopoly. Which of these motives drives Bill Gates? Serving consumers or monopolizing? With the entire legal profession's attention riveted, and much of the rest of the nation's besides, on the answer to that question, no one bothers to ask the only question that should matter to anyone concerned either about freedom or about business efficiency: Who cares? While some find it amusing or even career-enhancing to watch Bill Gates squirm under a David Boies cross-examination, or even more so to watch him try to counter the impression elicited by Mr. Boies that he is a disingenuous, predatory monopolist by singing "Twinkle, Twinkle, Little Star" for Barbara Walters (just as he does for his young daughter), the whole charade on all sides is distracting at best. Why aren't we rejoicing that it is so hard to tell the difference between serving consumers and monopolization? (The lawyers, of course, are rejoicing, but that's because their careers depend on teasing out the difference.) This should be a slam-dunk for any modern day Adam Smith to demonstrate how the invisible hand works such wonders, how having many such self-interested predators around can work to the benefit of all. Hasn't it occurred to anyone that the difficulty of distinguishing between these two is a sign that antitrust is flawed to the core, that here and perhaps in many other ways we are skewering those whose activities we should be commending?

The answer is that, while there are a few around who occasionally point out such things, so strong is the intellectual undertow generated by the denial defense, that even their voices are drowned out by the din of arguments shaped by the antitrust bar. In fact, the occasional glimpses of clarity are as often as not *drowned out by the very visionaries who offer them* as they struggle to gain credibility by taking up the conservative side of the denial defense. The situation has naturally set up a virtually infinite and still proliferating number of booby traps that catch and render even the most cogent insights irrelevant. The way it works is the following. Since many of the potential violations are related and often substitutes for each other, the permutations and combinations with which regulators can assemble a case are virtually infinite. And, since guilt or innocence frequently turns on such nebulous issues as whether the accused did or did not know what he

---

Reconsideration"), Microsoft was reported to be asking the Appeals Court to change its mind on its conclusion that " 'such commingling has an anticompetitive effect' [because] it deterred computer makers from installing browsers made by rivals." The company, perhaps put off balance by yet another word for the practice ("commingling"), said " 'Microsoft believes the district court's finding [which the Appeals Court confirmed] on this matter is clearly erroneous.' " Two weeks later the Times uses still another word for the practice in its report of the court's rejection of the company's request for reconsideration: "A federal appeals court refused yesterday to reconsider its ruling that Microsoft illegally blended Internet browsing software with its monopoly product, the Windows operating system." The New York Times article, "Court Again Rebuffs Microsoft on Bundling of Its Software," August 3, 2001.

was doing when he did (or didn't) do it, you can get sometimes the most ridiculously disingenuous denials and situations where the mood of the public or the court can make a big difference.[79] All of this affords both prosecutors more flexibility in bringing cases and defendants more flexibility to mount creative denials. The combination creates endless expansion of the varieties of arguments between hang-em-high liberals and get-em-off-the-hook conservatives. With so much real money on the line, the legal and academic professions tend to reward those who can make relevant arguments for any ongoing or future cases. Even conservatives who may be highly suspicious of the whole process, therefore, cannot have their ideas considered unless they get a toehold in the debate through some get-em-off-the-hook argument. Given the poor theorizing that led to antitrust in the first place, and the century of inconsistent application, any well-fed conservative can find at least some holes in every prosecutor's arguments. Still, as I said earlier, it is only the existence of these arguments that really matters, not who wins or loses. And the fact that they exist can only serve to strengthen the acceptance of antitrust. While the conservatives do gain their toeholds, any real freedom-based insights are so buried under get-em-off-the-hook arguments that the impact is to further empower antitrust, regardless of their content or cogency.

When ardent anti-antitrusters like Dominick T. Armentano argue, for example, that cartels are almost impossible to hold together,[80] or that tying agreements may not work,[81] the effect of these arguments is to underscore the impression that, if a monopolist *could* hold a cartel together, or *could* use tying to extend dominance from one product to another, doing so would be illegal, and perhaps appropriately so. So you can add these practices to the aforementioned predatory pricing as potential monopolization techniques that have become off limits precisely because of conservative arguments meant to help monopolists accused of them. Many of Armentano's arguments are based upon showing how difficult it is to monopolize, usually to imply that the things the laws are trying to prevent don't really happen much anyway. This kind of argument leaves conservatives completely exposed to the danger that, if monopolists ever do show up wanting to do all those things the conservatives have said are not worth the effort, the bureaucrats could hoist them on their own petard. As luck would have it, this is just what has happened.

---

[79] Judge Thomas Penfield Jackson's pique at the untrustworthiness of the Microsoft witnesses is a good example.

[80] "In short, it is probable that private price-fixing agreements would be unstable when [a variety of normal conditions occur]. Any of these factors might be enough to limit successful price collusion. And, since a great many markets, at one time or another, display these various conditions, it appears reasonable to assume that generally successful collusion would be of minor proportions even without antitrust prohibition." D. T. Armentano, *Antitrust and Monopoly; Anatomy of a Policy Failure*, 1982.

[81] "The fact remains that rivals can always attempt to compete in the tied-good market by simply lowering their prices in that market." D. T. Armentano, *Antitrust and Monopoly; Anatomy of a Policy Failure*, 1982.

While conservatives can hardly be blamed for trying to help monopolists where they can, they are now finding that the requisite focus on practical rather than principled criticism, on crafting aids for the denial defense rather than standing up for freedom, has painted them into a corner. Having now made the case that monopolies are so difficult to establish as to be not worth pursuing, along comes the Information Age and network effects, creating, in the words of a New York Times headline, a Land of Monopolies – and trouble.[82] In a moment we will see how conservatives now find themselves *locked in* to positions that are wrong on science, wrong on economics, and wrong on the law. (This is a fine irony, given conservatives' view that network effects and lock-in don't really exist.) Even if one grants their arguments as they may have applied to the Old World, the very pillars of their case make it imperative to bolster antitrust now. Before moving on to the network effect economy, let's briefly survey the state of play in antitrust debate.

That the antitrust laws were being inconsistently or incorrectly applied to the point that we might be better off without them was a position very nearly taken by Robert Bork in *The Antitrust Paradox*. In the end, his criticisms only served to help resolve some inconsistencies, such as that "efficient" combinations should not be barred, if they benefited consumers. Thus, his criticisms had the effect of solidifying support for antitrust even more than had he not made them. Bork is a noted conservative, of course; in fact, one of the best examples of orthodox conservatism you can find. He is also one of the best examples of orthodox antitrust views. As far as I can tell, he agrees in all material respects with Clinton Justice Department officials like Joel Klein and Janet Reno, as well as with fellow Chicago Schooler Richard Posner, an early advocate of deregulation. Deregulation is what you might call the "strong form" of antitrust, relying so much on the presumed robustness of antitrust theory that its advocates are confident they can even force "competition" on natural monopolies. Thus, on antitrust, the conservative Chicago position and the liberal view are one and the same and constitute, in effect, today's orthodox antitrust view.

But let's not forget the other schools mentioned earlier. Although their positions often seem to blend, or at least the conservatives in them seem to hold positions from several at once, the main contributions today are as follows. The Public Choice school criticizes the self-interest of bureaucrats, while sometimes participating in the bureaucratic process to devise more efficient structures. They are skeptical, based on the empirical evidence, that antitrust produces any benefits.

---

[82] "But whatever the answer in [the Microsoft] case, there is a growing realization among economists and technology experts that Microsoft may be only the most visible symptom of a problem afflicting the Internet economy. What troubles some observers of the world of Internet-enabled software and services – which marches to slogans like "get big fast" and "winner take all" – is that a number of factors make it a breeding ground for monopolies." The New York Times Week in Review article by John Schwartz "The Land of Monopolies," July 1, 2001.

Nonetheless, they hope that the institutions produced by open and honest debate will improve matters. Whether such improvements are labeled as reforms or as replacements of antitrust, they would clearly often be imposed from above, which would involve Government coercion. The Harvard School, which has been described as made up of "structuralists and their game theory descendents"[83] also would, it appears, impose deregulation schemes perhaps designed in the lab. In any case, they are advising many foreign countries on how to set up efficient antitrust structures, which presumably might include decentralized electronic trading systems, like those used in electric power deregulation here. Finally, the Austrian School, while the most philosophically pure on freedom, is – perhaps for that reason – seldom mentioned in today's antitrust debates.[84] Unfortunately, dismissing their guidance is made easier by the fact that many of their clearest voices – Mises, Hayek, Leoni, Rothbard – are no longer with us. This sad fact facilitates the cherry picking of their views by today's denial defense teams, seeking out, say, monopoly descriptions that can be turned into monopolization-is-difficult-and-therefore-not-worth-the-time arguments, rather than defenses of freedom that could have been used to justify monopolization outright. As described above in the discussion of Armentano, even a small amount of attention paid to an argument's denial defense utility can dilute and pollute its defense-of-freedom potential.

All of these schools are generally viewed as conservative, and all of them are inadvertently undermining the cause of freedom by implicitly endorsing antitrust's core principles. Liberals who support antitrust may be meddlesome, but they are not particularly damaging to freedom, since they are *always* in favor of intervention and, therefore, have limited intellectual credibility in the debate. Dealing with knee-jerk liberals from Marx on down is not the problem. The Trojan

---

[83] Fred S. McChesney and William F. Shughart II, *The Causes and Consequences of Antitrust, The Public Choice Perspective*, 1995.

[84] Actually, the Austrians have been ostracized right from the beginning, when Carl Menger and his followers in the latter decades of the 19th century developed models of human behavior based on subjective perceptions of value, such as might be determined by a good's *scarcity* or its *marginal utility*. These theories lent themselves to explaining the patterns of economic activity and the shapes of economic institutions based on individual choices between alternatives, rather than on the more fashionable notion that the value of a good derived from the labor and/or capital applied to its creation. But if, as Menger believed, the actual value of a good had nothing to do with its historical origin, it followed that there was no benefit and probably much harm that would come from any positivistic attempts to measure and address "mis-allocations," "inefficiencies" and the like. Obviously, this didn't sit well with interventionists, then or now. German economists of the dominant Historical School in Menger's time were confident in their policy prognoses, and resentful of Menger's implied criticism of their interventionism. Gustav Schmoller, the leading economist of the Historical School, "went so far as to declare publicly that members of the 'abstract' school were unfit to fill a teaching position in a German university, and his influence was quite sufficient to make this equivalent to a complete exclusion of all adherents to Menger's doctrines from academic positions in Germany." Hayek's introduction (1976) to an English translation of Carl Menger's *Principles of Economics* (1871). One wonders if the full flowering of historical positivism in Nazi Germany shortly after Menger's death in 1921 might have been mitigated if Schmoller's ostracism of Menger's disciples had not been so successful.

horse is the problem. As long as conservatives are arguing only over technicalities rather than principle, the overall effect is to strengthen antitrust. And as long as they grant its premises – even if only to gain traction for their get-em-off-the-hook arguments – they hammer home more firmly than any liberal could the impression that those premises are valid. Conservatives do the most damage to freedom, because they are the ones who would be expected to raise a note of caution over principle, if one were justified. Their failure to do so provides strong support to the assumption that Government intervention to restrain at least some kinds of monopolies is a good idea. And that's all the justification the bureaucrats need to erect the entire antitrust edifice.

Not only are conservatives who accept antitrust more damaging to freedom than liberals are, but the more libertarian a given conservative is, the more damaging are any antitrust arguments he makes – regardless of content – if they fail to simply reject antitrust as a violation of property and freedom. Take Jim DeLong, for example, a commentator for the Competitive Enterprise Institute who is regularly acerbic on antitrust, and the author of *Property Matters*, a fine expose of how liberals, environmentalists and other socialists are undermining property rights. But when summarizing the Appeals Court "victory" for Microsoft, he allows that "part of the opinion annoys those of us who think that the current antitrust doctrine about monopoly is in sad disrepair."[85] What else could the reader conclude but that DeLong – arch conservative and antitrust critic extraordinaire – believes antitrust can be repaired and, therefore, implicitly believes in antitrust? Precisely because he has made such incisive critiques of antitrust, DeLong's always implicit and sometimes explicit acceptance of its core principles is devastating for freedom.

Locked In

DeLong is probably as good a place as any to bring up the final straw for conservatives: the QWERTY Confusion. Here is how he sums up the issue:

> "[E]xamine the concept of 'lock in,' the idea that an inferior technology can get an advantage off the starting line and that thereafter society is 'locked in' to it, unable to change. But no one has found real-world examples. The cases usually cited are the adoption of the QWERTY keyboard over the Dvorak, and the triumph of the VCR over the Betamax home recorder. The validity of both these examples has been demolished, and substitute anecdotes have not yet

---

[85] James V. DeLong online commentary in CEI *Spin*, June 28, 2001.

been found. Similarly, 'network effects' are cited, and 'increasing returns to scale.' Again, however, real examples are hard to find." [86]

Or take Clyde Wayne Crews, current director of technology studies at the libertarian Cato Institute and, like DeLong, a commentator for the Competitive Enterprise Institute:

"Microsoft is bearing the brunt of this theory today. One cannot escape hearing the common claim that Microsoft's Windows was an inferior computer operating system to begin with, and that it won out over technologically superior competitors like Apple and IBM's OS/2 through luck and marketing. . . Without this foundation, most of today's antitrust attacks in the high-tech arena fall to the ground. . . As facts would have it, the world of inefficient technological lock-in is make-believe. Absent a government franchise that outlaws competition altogether, there are no credible instances of inferior products or technologies winning out and harming consumers through lock-in. As the pathbreaking work of economists Stan Liebowitz and Stephen Margolis has shown, even the most prominent examples of inefficient lock-in are invalid. They're simply myths. . . [T]he much-praised "Dvorak" typewriter keyboard layout was not superior to today's "Q-W-E-R-T-Y" keyboard configuration in objective typist-timing tests." [87]

And here is how Liebowitz and Margolis put it in several passages from *Winners, Losers and Microsoft*, the book that most comprehensively lays out the conservative view on lock-in:

"The very heart of our argument is that network effects do not 'protect' market participants from competition. The essence of the lock-in claim is that inferior products are 'protected' from superior newcomers. . . [T]here is neither convincing theory nor even minimal empirical support for the lock-in proposition." Or: "[N]ot even QWERTY offers us a QWERTY world and . . . other QWERTY worlds are awfully hard to find." Or: "These monopolies, we would argue, are efficient outcomes in network industries, where the network

---

[86] James V. DeLong, "Intellectual Property and Antitrust Enforcement"; House Oversight Hearing on the Antitrust Enforcement Agencies, April 12, 2000.
[87] CEI On Point article by Clyde Wayne Crews, Jr., "Network Effects: Does Luck or Talent Rule the High Technology Market," Febrary 27, 1998.

effect, or scale economy, is strong. It is not our argument that such monopolies would never arise, but rather that these monopolies would not be locked in. Such monopolies are serial monopolies; one monopoly after another." [88]

I hope after the earlier discussion that the reader can recognize the argument over lock-in as just another example of a denial defense debate, an argument between hang-em-high liberals and get-em-off-the-hook conservatives. Observe, for example, that – regardless of who is right on the science or the law – the effect of *arguing* that QWERTY is a myth is that, if any wannabe monopolist *could* ride network effects to durable lock-in, he *would be* guilty, or at least would have a much harder time proving his innocence. This is really just a more all-encompassing version of the predation arguments. In those, as you will recall, conservatives claim that predation doesn't work or isn't worth the time, in the hopes of persuading the court of the foolishness of the Government's case. But, win or lose, the effect of having made such an argument is to more firmly outlaw whichever predatory practice their client had been accused of – or any future client might be accused of.

Because network effects and lock-in, if valid concepts, make all kinds of predation easier to pursue, and more likely to pay predators for their time and effort, the theory in one fell swoop threatens to hoist all the previous get-em-off-the-hook arguers on their own petard. No wonder they are trying so hard to "debunk" it, "demolish" it, or declare it to be a "myth." And no wonder they all seem so anxious to confirm the success of each others' debunking, demolishing and de-mything. All the circular congratulation seems necessary because, if lock-in is real, predatory pricing to bump off a new competitor with temporary discounts so you can make more later, for example, will work quite well. So would bolting a free browser to your dominant operating system to kill off a competing platform. So would muscling OEMs to carry your OS exclusively so as to give an advantage to your applications software products. And so would bundling as many of those applications as possible into your OS so that the whole world of PC computing will have to march to your standard. Given the potential of lock-in theory to place previous and planned practices of Microsoft in a harsh monopolizing light, it is no wonder that the company backs the QWERTY-is-a-myth view.

Perhaps that's why the company has had Liebowitz and Margolis on the payroll as consultants at times during the '90s,[89] and has been a funding sponsor of

---

[88] Stan J. Liebowitz and Stephen E. Margolis, *Winners, Losers and Microsoft: Competition and Antitrust in High Technology*, 1999.
[89] Wall Street Journal review of *Winners, Losers and Microsoft* by Lee Gomes, "Bookshelf: The Truth About Marketplace Battles," August 26, 1999.

The Independent Institute, which published *Winners, Losers and Microsoft*. The company also secretly paid for full-page ads, nominally taken out by The Independent Institute, in which 240 academics signed onto the company's view without knowing it was funding the ad,[90] an embarrassing episode uncovered later by the trash-digging efforts of Larry Ellison's anti-Microsoft squad. The ads, the book and the QWERTY-is-a-myth theory were all meant to influence the court of Judge Thomas Penfield Jackson, who, in the end, was not impressed. Nor were the seven Appeals Court justices the case went to next who, whatever they thought of Judge Jackson's talking out of court, confirmed his monopolization conclusions.

The problem with this argument, legally, is that there is no mention of it in the antitrust laws. Nowhere does it say that monopolization is OK, provided your monopoly won't last very long, or if it is only one monopoly in a series of them that share the market sequentially. As much as academics would no doubt jump at the chance to develop statistical guidelines for *networkyness* or *seriality* to determine when we could excuse monopolization, the Hail Mary nature of the Microsoft strategy can easily be seen in a few not altogether tongue-in-cheek restatements of it: *Antitrust was and is based on sound theory, but now it is no longer needed, except to go after old companies.* Or how about this: *The reason antitrust is no longer needed is that companies are doing much more now of what we needed the law for before.* Or this: *The same process that made monopolies bad in the old days is now making them good.* And why? *Because there is so much more of that violative behavior now.* And how about this one: *Monopolization is happening so fast and furiously now that trustbusters needn't worry about it anymore.* All of these strange implied statements of QWERTY-is-a-myth doctrine are inevitable consequences of the denial defense in this case. By adopting this particular version, Microsoft forced itself into the weird position of having to argue that it was *not* a monopoly based on standards that don't exist yet, while supporting that assertion with a tacit admission that it *is* a monopoly by today's standards. And the fact that it was only through tacit admissions or "independent" third parties that the case could be made or the m-word mentioned was the cause of much hilarious disingenuousness on the part of Microsoft witnesses, and probably the most important factor that soured the public, the press, and Judge Jackson on the company. Having exhausted good will and credibility by denying that it was a monopoly, when its own arguments admitted by implication that it was, it was easy enough to convict the company on monopolization charges.

The problem with the argument economically is that *all* monopolies are temporary. At best, the serial monopoly distinction is a matter of degree, not kind – and an arbitrary one at that. How, for example, could we say that a 2-year

---

[90] New York Times article, "Microsoft Covered Cost of Ads Backing It in Antitrust Suit," September 17, 1999.

monopoly is OK, but one that lasts 3 years gets hit. At best these kinds of approaches to making the distinction required by the Microsoft argument would just add another dimension by which arbitrary bureaucrats could decide which are the good monopolies and which are the bad ones. And it would certainly ratchet up the hypocrisy and cynicism. How would you feel, for example, if companies that are obviously monopolizing like crazy got a pass, while trustbusters ticketed the slowpokes? That would be like having a traffic cop write you up for going 75 in a 60, while just watching as others zoomed by at over 100. So far, anyway, Judge Jackson and the seven justices of the DC Appeals Court have at least provisionally rejected Microsoft's logic, and have sounded more confused than persuaded by it.[91]

The final problem with QWERTY-is-a-myth is that it is almost certainly wrong on the science. I say this only partly because Liebowitz and Margolis seem forced, at least in their less guarded moments, to admit the truth of network effects, monopolization and lock-in even as they are devising denial defense arguments against them. [92] But the bigger hole in their case becomes visible when they try to argue, as part of the overall effort to minimize monopolization, that network effects do not result in lock-in, when what they really mean is that the lock-in is so brief that it shouldn't really matter. This may sound like a minor quibble, but it has major implications for the credibility and viability of their scientific and legal arguments. The way they phrase the issue enables them to make bold statements that there are no examples of *harmful* lock-in. While this is true, it is not because lock-in does not exist, as they argue, but because it does. There are plenty of ways that improvements can occur in spite of, and even because of, lock-in. Again, this is not just a quibble.

---

[91] The unanimous opinion of the seven justices of the Appeals Court for the District of Columbia Circuit, decided on June 28, 2001, touched on the network effect issue as follows: "Rapid technological change leads to markets in which 'firms compete through innovation for temporary market dominance, from which they may be displaced by the next wave of product advancements.' . . . Microsoft argues that the operating system market is just such a market. . . . *Whether or not Microsoft's characterization of the operating system market is correct does not appreciably alter our mission in assessing the alleged antitrust violations in the present case.* . . . The issue is particularly complex because, in network industries characterized by rapid innovation, both forces [those that could justify tougher enforcement, and those that could justify more lenient enforcement] may be operating and can be difficult to isolate. . . . Moreover, it should be clear that *Microsoft makes no claim that anticompetitive conduct should be assessed differently in technologically dynamic markets. It claims only that the measure of monopoly power should be different. For reasons fully discussed below, we reject Microsoft's monopoly power argument.*" [Edited for readability. Emphasis added.]

[92] "And anything that a firm does to improve its products, extend its standards, or reach additional markets will look like an attempt to monopolize. It will look like and attempt to monopolize because it *is* an attempt to monopolize. But where standards or networks or other sources of increasing returns are sufficiently important, such actions might be socially desirable. In fact, these actions are the very things that allow more valuable societal arrangements – standards, networks and new technologies – to replace less valuable ones." Stan J. Liebowitz and Stephen E. Margolis, *Winners, Losers and Microsoft: Competition and Antitrust in High Technology*, 1999. [Original emphasis].

The authors may not know it, but their way of putting the issue is inconsistent with these concepts that they appear to understand and, at least in the case of network effects, explicitly acknowledge believing in. In the first place, network effects and *potential* lock-in are inseparable. In tautological fashion, the network effect process inherently includes the possibility of multiple equilibriums and, therefore, inherently includes the possibility of *randomly* locking in to one of them. Randomness here precludes any certainty that the locked in technology is the best one of the multiple choices. And lock-in means that there will be at least *some* stickyness giving an advantage to a technology that is locked in over one that is not. How do Liebowitz and Margolis expect this blind process, of which there are many examples outside the economic realm, [93] to distinguish between technologies so that it would only lock in the good ones? Of course, there could be no such agent or force. Thus, it is inherently inconsistent with these concepts to expect consumer preferences or efficiency to immediately dissolve lock-in of an inferior technology. And it is absurd to conclude that, when the monopoly does turn over, the replacement will always and immediately be the very best of all possibilities. But both of these highly improbable outcomes would need to be proved to be always true if the Liebowitz/Margolis view on lock-in were valid. That would be tantamount to saying that these processes they acknowledge the existence of – don't really exist after all. So instead they say that they do exist, but don't really have the effects that their existence tautologically implies.

It may be worth observing that myths can be instructive, regardless of how much truth is behind them, as the mythologies of early civilizations, and maybe some religions today, demonstrate. The QWERTY story is particularly instructive, because, if it were true that it was deliberately designed to make typing harder (to prevent fast typists from making the keys stick, as the story goes), it would be a dynamite example of tipping and lock-in. Obviously, its lesson value is the reason it was so quickly accepted by network effect theorists, and perhaps why they may have done less basic fact-checking than Liebowitz and Margolis did. And any carelessness in this regard certainly would make it the perfect straw man for Liebowitz and Margolis to knock down. But what do the overblown claims of self-interested touters of alternative keyboard arrangements like August Dvorak, the Navy or Apple have to do with lock-in? While much of the authors' detail-digging

---

[93] "Of recent fascination to physical chemists, biologists, and economists are nonlinear dynamical systems of the 'dissipative' or 'autocatalytic' or 'self-reinforcing' type, where positive feedbacks may cause certain patterns or structures that emerge to be self-reinforcing. Such systems tend to be sensitive to early dynamical fluctuations. Often there is a multiplicity of patterns that are candidates for long-term self-reinforcement; the cumulation of small events early on 'pushes' the dynamics into the orbit of one of these and thus 'selects' the structure that the system eventually locks into." "This lock-in-by-fluctuation to one pattern or structure out of several possible has parallels in thermodynamics, ferromagnetism, laser theory, and chemical kinetics, and in allele fixation through genetic drift." W. Brian Arthur, *Increasing Returns and Path Dependence in the Economy*, 1994. Excerpts from chapters 3 and 7.

is directed to exposing the not particularly startling fact that salesmen will be salesmen, the leap made from there to the conclusion that QWERTY is not locked in is in no way supported by the exposé. Although the authors do demonstrate that QWERTY is probably about as good as any other arrangement and, therefore, is not an example of *bad* technology lock-in, the same evidence they marshal to make that claim actually confirms that QWERTY *is* locked in. If, as one study they quote – approvingly, because it helps make their case that QWERTY isn't inferior – says, "the layout of the keys makes surprisingly little difference," the fact that QWERTY has endured in the face of touters looking to topple it *confirms* lock-in. Particularly so, since those touters have been fully able to make use of the QWERTY myth in their pitches. In other words, the same widespread awareness of QWERTY's probable faults was used mercilessly by all the touters in their attempts to replace it. Yet QWERTY still stands and, according to Liebowitz' and Margolis' account, has never been seriously challenged. Based on the evidence they present, QWERTY is probably somewhere near the top of possible arrangements from an ergonomic efficiency standpoint, but even they don't claim it is the best. Because of its dominant position, however, it is virtually impossible to fully test or credibly introduce any alternative.

The authors boldly claim that their opponents' inability to prove that Dvorak is superior to QWERTY debunks the myth. It doesn't. Debunking requires a much harder test, one which they don't even attempt to meet. It requires proving that QWERTY is superior. They must not just show that there is *not* sufficient evidence to prove Dvorak is superior (which they do), but they must also show that there *is* sufficient evidence to prove that QWERTY is superior. And not just to Dvorak, but to all the other potential keyboard arrangements. (Brian Arthur puts the number of possible arrangements at 40-factorial, or 10 to the 48th.) I am not suggesting the authors should have tried to meet such a tough test. In fact, it will almost always be impossible to show that any given technology is superior to the nearly infinite alternatives that could conceivably replace it. But for that same reason, their challenge to the "QWERTY aficionados" to come up with a "single piece of support for the theory" [94] is a red herring. No one can ever *prove* that any technology, used or unused, incumbent or challenger is superior. There are simply too many complexities in every environment, too many times when an inefficiency from one perspective is an efficiency from another, too many unanticipated changes, unanticipated uses, unintended consequences. Speculations regarding the relative efficiencies of technology alternatives make for interesting discussion, and

---

[94] Demonstrating that they haven't changed their minds since the book came out, in a chat thread revealed on a Google search of "QWERTY, Network Effects, Lock-in" (1080 hits, July 16, 2001), Liebowitz says: "QWERTY economics is a new theory. The old theory generally worked pretty well. QWERTY aficionados believe we should have the government act on the basis of these theories. All we are asking is a single piece of support for the theory."

occasionally create exciting opportunities for capital to chase. But any "conclusions" reached are inherently tentative and, therefore, say nothing about the truth or falsehood of lock-in theory.

An important corollary of this thought is that *all* incumbent technologies, products or institutions are less than perfect; there is *always* something better out there. Thus it may be true, trivially, when Brian Arthur says, "The 1950s programming language FORTRAN, the U.S. color television system and the QWERTY typewriter keyboard are demonstrably inferior structures that seem to be locked in," but so what? Every technology can be improved and is, therefore, "demonstrably inferior." And every incumbent technology has some stickyness or lock-in to it. But that is no reason to connect the two thoughts, as Arthur does, to build a case for Government intervention to break up lock-in situations. In fact, the opposite is true: Capital chasing new lock-in opportunities is certainly the best driver of the dissolution of old ones. The last thing we should do if we want to foster efficient turnover of locked in technologies is to get Government involved in removing the lock-in incentive. Especially since by thus emasculating capital we would be left with no choice but to let Government planners make all the selections for us.

The implication here for Liebowitz, Margolis and Microsoft is that they have their strategy exactly backwards. Network effects and lock-in do exist and that is why Microsoft managed to lead the greatest economic advance in the history of civilization. And it is because they do exist that greater antitrust intervention is a bad idea. Rather than trying to attack Klein, Arthur & Co. on the basics of law and science – a fool's errand if ever there was one – a straightforward defense based on the value of monopolization might have had some chance of allowing them to continue in the same direction. On the current track, in contrast, the denial defense is blocking any chance that they will be able to pull that trick again. While Wintel worked wonders, nothing on the drawing board now, nor anything else they might dream up, has any chance of doing something similar in the future. Not Hailstorm, not dot-Net, and not any further bundling into the OS or browser or any other platform. That is because the denial defense has prevented Microsoft from honestly defending its monopolization. And its disingenuous denials have alerted the company's friends and the Feds to that monopolization, causing the former to lose sympathy for the company, [95] and giving the latter a roadmap to violations.

---

[95] New York Times Op-Ed, "The Smell Test," by Paul Krugman, July 1, 2001. "Now for the bad news. Even as this case was working its way through the courts, Bill Gates and Steve Ballmer were still up to their old tricks. The next Microsoft operating system, Windows XP, contains Windows Media Player, which – unlike AOL's RealPlayer – apparently will play music and video in Microsoft's proprietary formats but not in those of competitors. Now I have generally felt that Microsoft gets a worse rap than it deserves, and I criticized Judge Jackson's breakup plan from the start. But this looks like sheer arrogance – the sort of arrogance that got Microsoft in trouble in the first place. That arrogance is what drove Judge Jackson over the edge. He concluded that Mr. Gates and his friends could not be

Therefore, if any of their new initiatives do begin to succeed like the old, they will get re-busted.

If Liebowitz and Margolis would still like an example of lock-in, how's this: The Denial Defense. I don't believe any other approach, such as the honest defense of monopolization I have recommended here, was considered, either by Microsoft, or by any other company I have read about who was accused of antitrust violations. Why? Because all the players are locked in to the Denial Defense. Without adhering to it, the lawyers and academics would have no careers; the politicians would not be able to fulminate and fluster over greed and unfairness and, thus, would not get elected; the state attornies general would not get on the evening news and have a shot at becoming governors or senators; the companies would not have a shot at their Billion Dollar Pot-o'-Rent; and the bureaucrats would have to fold up their tent and go home. So it is no wonder that alternative strategies are never considered and the Denial Defense and antitrust generally become ever more locked in.

As to whether the socialism it represents is the most efficient organizing institution that we as a society could adopt, well, after what I've said here, I guess I can't claim I can *prove* there is a better alternative. But I can say unequivocally that, as a matter of political choice, we Americans *believe* there is a better alternative, and we have long since decided to go with it. Sure, there are eighty countries out there now with antitrust laws. Fine. By all means, let one hundred socialisms bloom; just let them bloom somewhere else. For better or worse, America was founded on freedom. It is simply not a competitive option for *this* country in the 21st century to abandon its principles, even if socialism is a better idea. Even if antitrust and deregulation could in some sense "work" economically, the loss of freedom required for their implementation is terminally inconsistent with who we think we are as a people. And even if freedom is flawed, or is somehow no longer viable in a country as mature and rich as ours, we still have no choice but to reaffirm our commitment to it. It should be obvious that *I* don't think freedom is flawed. And it is clear that the majority of Americans agree, if for no other reason than that the political popularity of deregulation stems from the promise in the word that its implementation is an uptick for freedom. Of course, a freedom that could admit such a corrosive Trojan horse into its inner sanctum would indeed be flawed. I do hope, however, that there is a way to reaffirm our commitment to freedom, to expose and banish the traitor in our midst, and to move forward in a principled way that would make our Founders proud.

---

trusted, that they would always try to find a way around any court order that limited their conduct, and that the only way to enforce good behavior was a drastic "structural" remedy. It's now up to Microsoft to prove that he was wrong. Otherwise, we'll see them back in court – and the next judge will keep his mouth shut but carry a big stick."

If it turns out in the end that freedom is not long-term viable after all, well, c'est la vie. At least we would have given it our best shot according to our deepest moral beliefs and traditions. Freedom is the one unique thing we Americans do better and more powerfully than anyone else. Socialisms are a dime a dozen in today's world. If we went down fighting for freedom, that is to say, organizing our economic and social lives again according to Individual Liberty and the Rule of Law, I think most Americans would accept that, however sadly. But if we go down because we can't resist those politically correct socialisms so popular everywhere else, well that would truly be a tragedy for a country founded on freedom. And what the hell: Even if we do have to turn to socialism eventually, at least we'll have a lot of experimental versions to choose from. But for now there is no reason not to give freedom another chance.

Repealing all antitrust laws is the most important step this country could take in the direction of freedom. Given the political and philosophical lock-in of these excuses for intervention, however, I have little hope that any debate over repeal could do anything but further lock them in. That is because they would inevitably be debated on the merits, the pros and cons vis-a-vis efficiency, fairness etc. of each element of the antitrust corpus that would be removed by repeal. And, like every other argument over the details of antitrust, such debates would only strengthen its grip. The only chance, as I see it, to overcome inertia here is to go over the heads of the bureaucrats and others who are locked in to antitrust by creating a legal or constitutional ban on the kind of intrusive Government coercion the implementation of antitrust requires. Such a ban would inevitably have major effects not just on antitrust but on Government generally – largely by drastically shrinking its size and scope – and would thus be challenged furiously by all who administer and receive Government benefits. I believe the needed restraint is consistent, however, not only with what people want as individuals, but with the kind of nation our Founders envisioned. What I have in mind is discussed next in robinhood.gov.

robinhood.gov

"Every election is an advance auction
on the sale of stolen goods."
- H. L. Mencken

What do ECNs, CLECs and ESCOs[96] have in common? They are all new businesses created out of thin air by deregulation. Of course the regulators don't incorporate these new businesses in any direct way themselves. Rather, their rules have the effect of ringing a come-and-get-it dinner bell, inviting everybody and his uncle to line up for a slice of a busted monopoly's business. The monopolists are required to give up the right to use or dispose of their property as they see fit, or to deny its use to others, thus losing all three of the options normally available to property owners. Most gallingly from their perspective, they are required to let the new competitors hook up to and use their networks, which were their main assets, indeed, their raison d'être. [97] Thus, amidst all the excitement about "competition," it is important to remember that antitrust always involves the confiscation and redistribution of property. The new competitors, for their part, have a very simple and attractive business plan. It is, with Government blessing, to steal and sell the monopoly's product to the monopoly's customers. The rules prevent the monopolies from stopping the looting or retaliating against the looters.

Of course, Government often transfers property or economic advantage from one party to another, and not just via antitrust. Patents being granted or going generic, environmental rules that bar landowners from using their own land, taxes

---

[96] ECNs are Electronic Communication Networks competing with the old stock exchanges. CLECs are Competitive Local Exchange Carriers competing with the old Baby Bells. ESCOs are Energy Service Companies competing with the old utilities.

[97] In practice the monopolies resist the confiscation, often with considerable success. The Baby Bells with their last mile monopolies, for example, frustrate their wannabe competitors and regulators by being less than forthcoming in providing connections or reasonable in pricing them. But, in the end, Government usually gets its way by breaking up or threatening to break up the recalcitrant ones. In a telling role reversal, AT&T is now one of the supplicants begging for antitrust breakups to get a piece of a monopoly's business. "Earlier this month, Republican Sen. Ted Stevens introduced legislation backed by AT&T Corp. that would break up so-called Bell companies such as Verizon Communications. A few hours after doing so, Mr. Stevens boarded a plane to his home state of Alaska for a fishing trip with AT&T's chief executive, C. Michael Armstrong. Mr. Stevens's support represents a rare success for AT&T in its struggle to forge closer ties with lawmakers and regulators as part of its campaign to break into the Bells' markets. The long-distance company, seeking to enter a branch of familiar territory after a failed foray into cable, argues that the Bells unfairly dominate local telephone-service markets. AT&T and other Bell opponents propose a radical solution: splitting the Bells into separate retail and wholesale divisions, or even into two stand-alone companies." The Wall Street Journal article, "AT&T Ratchets Up Efforts in Washington Pushing Bell Breakup Plan," August 28, 2001.

that turn into transfer payments, etc. A complete list would run to thousands of programs and hundreds of millions of individuals and companies whose economic prospects are reshuffled by deliberate or accidental Government action. It is my goal in this final chapter to suggest a means of preventing such transfers. And I mean *all* such transfers. We will find that the best means of preventing any confiscations is to prevent all of them. While I can't claim to have done anything like a thorough survey of what the effects of preventing Government from shuffling property would be, from a libertarian standpoint all the ones I have thought of so far seem pleasing. But I make no bones about it: My main goal is to prevent antitrust. If I am right that all antitrust involves property transfers, then preventing such transfers should do the trick – and do it without the Sisyphean chore of arguing over the pros and cons of each policy.

I harbor no illusions. Even without the Sisyphean chore, the task appears, and probably is, impossible. Nonetheless, it seems to me that now is the time for radical suggestions. Our nation has long since left the slippery slope and is plunging headlong into a socialist abyss. And, leading superpower that we are, we are taking the rest of Western Capitalism with us. Mine is not the first, and perhaps not the best, of the radical suggestions that have been thrown at this problem. But the more I look at the others, the more they appear both harder to implement and less effective than my suggestion, even though mine is far more radical. Before looking at our suggestions, let's see why we must find a means to simultaneously attack *all* interventionist takings, rather than beginning only with one, or a few, or only the weakest, or only antitrust.

Why Not Go After Antitrust?

Repealing the antitrust laws is the most important thing that could be done in the direction of restoring property rights. First of all, the antitrust takings are the largest. And, because the example set by antitrust lends legitimacy to all the others, its elimination would have wide-ranging indirect as well as direct benefits. Unfortunately, however, debates over repeal would only strengthen its hold. To give a one-sentence summary of the argument in Chapter 1: debates over the details of each policy, one by one, only contribute to the impression that antitrust has been thoroughly vetted and, therefore, strengthen it. Any debates over repeal would consist primarily of such arguments. There is no chance, therefore, to topple antitrust alone, because its rationale already includes the anti-antitrust side of the previous debates, which it has implicitly incorporated as "noted," and thereby rejected.

In addition, as a matter of political strategy, going after only one part of Government's fairness enterprise, such as antitrust, would expose the effort to probably fatal, though only implicit, charges of philosophical inconsistency. Fairness, after all, is a property that compels consistency by its nature. How could you be fair to some and not others without undermining the very concept? An attack on antitrust alone, therefore, would generate an implicit charge of unfairness. That the charge, being implicit, would only effect sentiment, rather than present an explicit intellectual challenge to repeal, would make it all the more devastating to any repeal effort. Because antitrust is certainly the least understood and, perhaps for that reason, the most widely supported of the interventionist rationales, the emotional backlash would be fearsome. The public would have no way of grasping the esoteric and technical case for repeal, but would understand only too well that very rich people and very large companies are the ones in favor of it. *Of course those greedy bastards don't want fairness to apply to* them – *you wouldn't either if you had* their *money.* In such an atmosphere, an attack on antitrust alone would be easily countered by demagogue-ing the "fat-cats" behind it who, without hope of reinforcements from other parties aggrieved by takings, would be left twisting in the wind.

Even more frail would be efforts to effect the piecemeal repeal of antitrust, beginning with its weakest elements. Bork, for one and Crews, for another, for example, have pointed to the Robinson-Patman price discrimination statute as a good place to begin reform or repeal,[98] since it causes much harm and does no good. Moreover, according to Bork, all "respectable scholarship" agrees.[99] But any effort to eliminate it – whether or not such effort is successful – would certainly have a negative effect on the effort to get rid of antitrust generally. First of all, price discrimination is a paradigmatic issue for demonstrating how antitrust debates can get bogged down in emotional arguments over fairness. It's got that ugly word – "discrimination" – to deal with, and what could be more unfair than selling the same product at different prices to different people? These problems mean that, however any debates play out, repeal advocates will need to do plenty of groveling at the feet of the fairness god to avoid the impression that they are just another special interest. It is precisely because of such requisite nods to the prevailing wisdom on antitrust's core principles that arguments over particular aspects of it cause antitrust to become more firmly established. Keep in mind that Bork is a firm defender of antitrust's core principles and has already contributed greatly to its strengthening by cleaning up inconsistencies around the edges. Robinson-Patman is, according to Bork, just another such inconsistency that has

---

[98] "Robinson-Patman could be a key test case for pursuing *reform* of antitrust legislation." Clyde Wayne Crews, Jr., "The Antitrust Terrible 10 – Why the Most Reviled 'Anti-competitive' Business Practices Can Benefit Consumers in the New Economy," Cato Policy Analysis No. 405, June 28, 2001. [Emphasis added.]

[99] "If that law is mistaken in its assumptions and further deformed in its application, as almost all respectable scholarship finds it [Robinson-Patman] to be, the needless deformation of market processes and the destruction of national wealth is enormous." Robert H. Bork, *The Antitrust Paradox – A Policy at War with Itself*, 1978.

taken antitrust away from its original consumer welfare goal. And Crews, although he questions the consumer benefits of many of those core principles, still is looking only for weak links to attack to begin the reform process. But the problem with these approaches is that the price of repealing the weak links is an implicit promise to bow all the more obsequiously before the strong ones. Thus, any approach to repeal, whether piecemeal or en masse, if it is based on the pros and cons of each policy separately, will not only fail, but will backfire by making antitrust stronger.

This is not say that continued sniping at its flaws is a bad idea. If and when some other approach shows promise, it will be beneficial to have made the case that antitrust will not be missed – indeed, that its withdrawal will cause citizens to rejoice as if freed from an occupying army. But tying any such critical analyses to a specific repeal plan will only undermine the credibility of the points of criticism, and would set back actual chances of repeal. And this is the best that can be expected, and even this would only occur if the criticisms did not include too many "denial defense" arguments designed to get clients off the hook in court (see Chapter 1, "Out of Order"). If they did, then even well-targeted sniping could hurt the cause, by once again expanding the range of opinion that can be included in the foundation of antitrust. Crews and Levy, for example, offer recent arguments that there are 10 (Crews) or 7 (Levy) reasons to reform or repeal antitrust.[100] Some of the reasons are valid and well argued; Levy, for example makes the bald assertion that antitrust should go because it "debases the idea of private property." But both include some standard denial defense arguments, such as QWERTY-is-a-myth. And, because both cases are built on an apparent need to get Microsoft off the hook, one gets the feeling that all the arguments amount to special interest pleading and, therefore, have limited potential to result in direct hits on antitrust's theoretical foundation. While these calls for repeal, as well as some others I have come across from the Public Choice or Austrian schools, are in some ways encouraging to the libertarian in me, I suspect that attaching them to any specific repeal effort could pose dangers. In short, the more components to the argument, the greater the chance that at least some element of antitrust will remain after "repeal." And the entire thing could regenerate, of course, from any single fragment. Indeed, after surviving "repeal," it would soon grow far larger and stronger than ever. Anyway, thoughts of repealing part or all of antitrust are just idle speculation. The most likely scenario is that the repeal flight would never leave the ground, but rather, like Bork's *Antitrust Paradox*, lead to reforms that give it greater theoretical consistency and strength.

---

[100] Clyde Wayne Crews, Jr., "The Antitrust Terrible 10 – Why the Most Reviled 'Anti-competitive' Business Practices Can Benefit Consumers in the New Economy," Cato Policy Analysis No. 405, June 28, 2001. Robert A. Levy, senior fellow at the Cato Institute, "The Microsoft Moral – Repeal the antitrust laws, for starters," The American Spectator Magazine, May 2000.

Why Not Go After Taxes, The Deficit, Affirmative Action?

The kind of resistance that would meet any effort to repeal antitrust can be expected from *every* effort to repeal *any* element of the Government Fairness Enterprise. All of them are susceptible to the appearance of special interest pleading and, thus, can be stopped cold by demagogue-ing. Some get special reputations as "third rail" situations, like Social Security, and all of them exhibit arguments between liberals defending and trying to expand them, and conservatives trying to cut them back a little. But, just as such arguments increase the acceptance of antitrust, the conflict over details only makes all these other programs stronger, too. The debate over whose Medicare prescription drug program should prevail, for example, only makes the continuance of Medicare itself more certain. The conflict over which Social Security reform to use makes it more likely that Social Security will continue. Even ending "Welfare as we know it" with "workfare," which has been a resounding success,[101] has made it *more, not less*, likely that Welfare will continue. And the conflicts over cutting taxes, over eliminating preferences in Government contracts, or over reining in affirmative action, only make it *more, not less,* likely that Government will stay involved in such property allocation exercises.

Since Ronald Reagan left office, conservative Republicans have caught themselves in one trap after another that has damaged their cause as their leaders have schooled the troops in how to couch cuts in liberal language. From President Bush senior's call for a "kinder and gentler" America, through Newt Gingrich's Class of '94 that promised to "reform" or "save" programs with cuts, to President Bush junior's "compassionate conservatism," not a single conservative leader has ventured to tell the truth. Their word waffles imply correctly that liberals have won the ideological war.[102] The only hope for conservatives, they seem to say, is to try to rein in the Welfare State surreptitiously by *sneaking in* measures that may have the *unrecognized* effect of slowing its growth. In the process they have given the

---

[101] The New York Times article, "2-Parent Families Rise After Change in Welfare Laws," August 12, 2001. Although the preliminary results imply strongly that, just as Welfare critics have always said, the payments were destroying families and creating a permanent, poverty-stricken underclass, the lesson drawn will almost certainly be that Government help in the transition to work and maybe Government "work" itself will be needed. The knee-jerk assumption that continued Government monitoring and assistance is needed to make workfare work will prevent any consideration of the obvious solution to the whole problem: eliminate all such programs entirely.

[102] The New York Times article, "President Asserts Shrunken Surplus May Curb Congress" August 25, 2001. "Mr. Bush avoided specific answers to several questions about how he would find the money for his next big initiatives, from missile defense, to overhauling the military, to reforming Medicaid, without dipping into Social Security surpluses that both parties have declared off limits. And he made it clear he would not re-think his tax cut, saying, "I can't tell you how proud I am to be traveling around the country and people say, 'Thanks for the $600.' ""

impression – again, correct – that their real agenda is to aid their supporters: Big Business, Big Oil, Big Drugs and wealthy and productive people, generally. In so doing, they have forfeited whatever claim they might have had to an ideologically pure reputation. Instead, even the wealthy have become just another interest group seeking to wangle some advantages out of the tax committees and rule-making bureaucracies. Just as both sides in an antitrust trial must assume the legitimacy of basic antitrust doctrine to gain any traction for their arguments, all political positions start from the assumption that Government should be in the business of allocating fair outcomes. Thus, the very process of conservative-versus-liberal argument causes the philosophical content of conservatism to blend indistinguishably into the general rent-seeking melee, in which disingenuous dodges are standard. Here, the name of the game is projecting images: of fairness, of caring, of knowledgeable, thoughtful, deliberative leaders balancing the competing claims and deciding what is right for us. The politician who does not accept the premise that doing good things for the people is what politicians should be doing has no chance of getting elected, and no chance of getting benefits for his constituents. Because conservatives are the ones who would be expected to reject such calculus, if rejection were justified, their failure to do so hammers home more firmly than any liberal could the assumptions behind the Welfare State.

Typical of the damage from conservative calumnies was that brought about by the deficit debacle. This began when waves of recruits using Gingrich's how-to-get-elected videotapes were swept into a House majority in 1994 based primarily on the promise to use the need to reduce the deficit as the excuse to cut programs. They didn't put it that way, of course. The videotapes taught them how to position what they were doing as a way to *save* the programs. They styled the cuts as unfortunately needed ones in otherwise good and well-intentioned programs. Not a single conservative said these programs should not be funded no matter how much money we had. Not a single one said that their very existence was a violation of property and freedom. They didn't say these things, because they would not have gotten elected if they did. But it was a Faustian bargain, making the implosion of the conservative majority inevitable from the moment it began. Even before the deficit disappeared, they were clearly fingered by the press and the people as more interested in swinging money from the poor to the rich than in saving or reforming the programs, and – like all politicians – willing to be thoroughly dishonest to achieve their ends. What could be more dishonest than taking money out of poverty programs under the guise of trying to save them? Of course, their arguments came back to haunt them, once the deficit issue turned into a surplus problem. By then, there was no more credible evidence that those programs were valuable than that *even conservatives* had said so.

After the deficit debacle, the perennial conservative ploy of tax cuts has had a harder time, because cuts have been easier to portray as just another giveaway to the wealthy. And this concern has made it particularly difficult to consider serious marginal rate relief, much less flat tax proposals. That's too bad, because the flat tax could go well beyond its economic effects to symbolically illustrate a point for freedom. Because it would treat all citizens equally, and would have the side effect of taking most or all of the special interest loopholes out of the code, the flat tax is consistent with the Rule of Law. And getting rid of loopholes would also jettison a great deal of the special interest pleading, lobbying and logrolling that politicians engage in. That, of course, is why it will almost certainly never pass. And, even if it did, like every other piecemeal reform, passage would be bought at the cost of conceding greater credibility to the other means by which politicians bestow favors, both through the tax code and through all the other benefit programs. The flat tax itself would almost certainly include large deductions for the first, say, $30,000 of income, and one or two traditional loopholes, like home mortgage interest. And no doubt the horse trading to get the votes for passage would include acquiescence in the maintenance or expansion of other programs favored by liberals.

Worst of all, the rationales offered in support of the flat tax will steer clear of outright claims of the illegitimacy of Government taking more from one man than from another. Rather, to avoid riling the socialist levelers, the focus will be on efficiency, incentives and other more technical arguments, such as supply-side economics. This failure to straightforwardly address the differential confiscation problem will not only leave intact the egalitarian ethic, which says that Government should *do something* about economic inequality, but will strengthen it. Even if by some miracle a flat tax passed, sooner or later it would re-occur that one of the best ways to address inequality is through the tax code. And any success it had had in the meantime that might be attributable to efficiency or whatever would be quickly forgotten. Supply-side theories, after all, even after being largely responsible for two decades of economic boom, are more derided than defended now in public debate. That those who always called them "trickle down economics" have the upper hand now is apparent in the conservatives' continued frantic search for ways to cut the liberals' programs without saying explicitly that they are doing so, much less explaining why freedom requires it.

Conservative evasions are proof positive that we are in a powerful positive feedback loop that is digging us deeper and deeper into a socialist grave. There is no program with enough corruption, waste and abuse that repealing it is politically possible. There is no price support inefficient enough or bureaucracy bumbling enough that a vote-seeking politician can realistically take it on. And even if he did, the result would almost certainly be another setback, both because he would lose, and because the effort to raise support for repeal of any one program would require concessions on the others that would effectively sell out any shot at attacking them. Thus, the net effect of any attempt to rein in socialism is stronger socialism. There is simply no policy or position that conservatives can realistically adopt that doesn't dig us in deeper, no matter how much they position themselves as anti-Washington. Such grandstanding rarely has any positive effect. And, by teaching supporters to camouflage their conservatism, as Newt Gingrich and the Presidents Bush have done, conservative leaders since Reagan have blown the chance to honestly make their case. So the public debate over cutting programs inevitably leads to greater acceptance of egalitarian theory – and the programs.

robinhood.gov

The most important reason for this decay of freedom is that today – Constitution or no – there are no effective restraints on the power of Government. Even the most junior Senator has more patronage power than the kings of old in terms of his or her ability to reward supporters as they jointly "fight the special interests." Whether they fight for "our children," for "working families," "the family farm," "working women" or any of the thousands of other categories or causes that politicians can attach themselves to, it is now universally believed that this is what politicians are *supposed* to do. That is, they are supposed to do good things for us, to fight effectively for our slice of the pie. Their credentials for doing so are ostensibly moral; they are assumed to have the right egalitarian attitudes and to be courageously and fairly trying to order the Government and our environment for the greatest good. But the moral claim is phony as a three-dollar bill. These are the same morals that led to the great evils of the twentieth century, to Hitler, Stalin, Mao and Pol Pot. The view is that trampling on individual rights is OK as long as it's for a worthy cause. But *this* is the road to serfdom. That we haven't gone far enough down it yet to see where it's heading does not mean that we are not on it, and traveling fast.

The best face that can be put on our politicians' moral claim is that they are acting like official Robin Hoods, taking from the rich to give to the poor. But where would Robin's reputation be today if, instead of braving the rigors of a highwayman in Sherwood Forest, he lived in a lavish castle and had the Sheriff of Nottingham's men at his disposal to simultaneously take taxes from all property owners? What if he and the Sheriff had used the proceeds primarily to bribe voters to keep themselves in power? And how would we feel if they had determined on their own how much and what types of property to take, and from whom, and where the proceeds would be most effectively spent as bribes? Even though we have not yet gone far enough down this road to see before us the clear outlines of tyranny, we are far enough along already that the U.S. Government could be thought of as the largest criminal enterprise in human history – call it "robinhood.gov." Its main activity is the ongoing confiscation of property – to the tune of trillions – and the co-opting of every individual citizen's ability to pursue happiness. The politicians figure they are morally covered provided they take testimony from enough industrial organization experts, enough environmental scientists, enough bio-ethicists etc, to make sure it appears as if the proceeds from their confiscations are spent for the greatest good. And they further justify the ostensible morality of their ministrations by constantly parading victims before the cameras on Capitol Hill to show us how much good they are doing. Victims of this, that and the other disease; of this, that and the other privation; of this, that and the other discrimination – and on and on it goes. They do all of this under the entirely false assumption that only Government can do such good things as provide economic openings for the downtrodden, or discover cures for diseases with stem cell research.

The much-noted decline of morals in America has its roots in acceptance of the theft-to-bribe model of Government, and not just because it routinely accepts theft and other violations of individual property rights. The egalitarian ethic underlying the model also requires the suspension of personal morals in service of non-discriminatory Government-defined values. Discrimination, the ability to decide with whom one associates – and with whom one *refrains* from associating – is the primary mechanism through which values are developed, defined, refined and enforced. It is the carrot and stick for good and bad behavior, and the mechanism underlying marriage, family, religion and all felicitous social organization. Because discrimination is the basis for the development and enforcement of morals, the entire anti-discrimination apparatus of Government is anti-morality. And there is a positive feedback loop operating here too, as every claim for "justice" leads to larger and larger counterclaims, causing the decline into the immorality of Government solutions to lead to more such declines. Just as antitrust lawyers must accept antitrust to gain relevance for their arguments, everyone at all levels of debate on all topics in America today starts by accepting the basic moral legitimacy of Government's confiscation-to-do-good role. And doing good on Government's terms always involves the equal, non-discriminatory distribution of the spoils of confiscation. So, if you thought you owned a building or a business, for example, and figured you would rent to or hire people you like – and refuse people you despise – think again. Government effectively owns your property, and will prevent you from exercising your basic right of discrimination with respect to it. Even if your religion tells you that homosexuality is wrong, for example, you will not be allowed to refuse to rent to or hire someone on that basis. It is difficult to overestimate the disorganizing effect that such strictures, multiplied millions upon millions of times a day in each community across the country, have on the disintegration of morals. Even if you would have agreed 99.99% of the time with the Government's choice, the fact that it is never *your* choice gradually forces you to abdicate moral responsibility for making it. And the cumulative effect of all these individual abdications drags the whole society down in terms of its power to discriminate between good and evil.

In the great stem cell debate leading up to President Bush's decision on August 9, 2001, for example, the entire argument on all sides was based on the premise that Government *should be* spending tax money on scientific research. No one questioned the right of Government to take money from citizens and spend it on science.[103] Never mind that the exercise of that role violates the basic principles of freedom and property our nation was founded on. Never mind that application of those funds offends the deepest moral beliefs of some of its citizens. Never mind that similar degrees of Government control over property, science and ethics led quickly to the horrors of Nazi Germany. The only issue today seems to be: How do we fine-tune our moral algorithms to maximize the expenditure of these public funds to do the greatest good? Given the moral morass that sole focus on that question fosters, is it any wonder that some today cannot even tell the difference between people dying in gas chambers and cells dying in test tubes?[104] With such deranged moral compasses, how could we expect to resolve any of the other moral issues of the day? As long as every Government program is potentially money well spent on good intentions, the only questions, morally, revolve around how to prioritize the taking and the spending. This is the real *war of all against all*. And it is an essentially evil enterprise, no matter what the bio-ethicists or Government-appointed moral pundits try to tell us.[105]

The existence of this war, started and sustained by Government's slice-and-dice role, is the primary fact of political life today. Even those who sense or

---

[103] The New York Times op-ed by President Bush, "Stem Cell Science and the Preservation of Life," August 12, 2001. "Government has a clear duty to promote scientific discovery – and a duty to define certain boundaries: Under my policy, existing stem cell lines, to be used in publicly supported research, must be derived (1) with the informed consent of donors, (2) from excess embryos created solely for reproductive purposes and (3) without any financial inducements to the donors."

[104] The New York Times article, "Abortion Foes Split Over Plan On Stem Cells; Bush's Decision Divides Realists and Purists," August 12, 2001. " 'The president's position contradicts the Nuremberg Code,' said Wendy Wright, the communications director of Concerned Women for America, a conservative public policy group. 'We should be horrified at the prospect of participating in research on embryos who are deliberately killed for the same reason that we are horrified that gold fillings were taken from the teeth of Holocaust victims.' "

[105] The Wall Street Journal article, "Bioethics Appointee Says He Is No Indoctrinator," August 17, 2001. I take from the article that our new ethics czar, Leon Kass, likes to think of himself as hard to pin down on moral issues, probably making him the ideal appointment for an age of diversity and moral equivalency. His egalitarian credentials are burnished by his rationale for opposing public eating – "people who do it don't usually offer to share" – and by his insistence that that view does not reflect any "aristocratic priggishness" on his part. Fairness fanatics will be further reassured by the fact that "In his earlier life, his sympathies were socialistic; in the mid-1960s he worked for civil-rights causes."

recognize its basic illegitimacy have no choice but to suck it up – and beg for their piece of the action. In other words, we must all stop whining about the loss of freedom and our basic rights of association and moral choice, and start whining with the rest of them on behalf of our own bigger slice. Every one of us has potential claims to more based on our membership in potentially favored groups. Getting more just involves a little bit of organizing and a lot of demonstrating, donating, lobbying, logrolling and generally loud whining. No one can doubt the success at winning special treatment of the most visible groups in recent decades: working women winning legal rights to quicker jobs and promotions, and protection against sexual harassment and "hostile environments;" blacks to affirmative action in hiring, contracting and school admissions; homosexuals to special non-discriminatory treatment in housing and employment, and to greater funding for medical expenditures to cure AIDS; the disabled who have the ADA to get special facilities in every building, and Government to override the rules of the Professional Golf Association.

Not to be outdone, conservatives have joined the chorus of whiners on behalf of families, entrepreneurs, science, economic progress, and soccer moms. Usually camouflaging their efforts behind phrases no one can understand and pushing them with appointees of unknown views (because that is the only way they can get confirmed), they try to roll back or prevent the worst of the confiscations. And conservatives know better than to position their claims as a repudiation of Government's redistributionist role. Instead, they have focused on getting their own slice of the distribution by pointing out the unfairness of taking property from productive people who also have mouths to feed, kids to send to college, and charity donations to make. In other words, they too whine. Why? Because win or lose, open or hidden, the fact is that whining works. Conservatives, liberals, *everybody* does it. There is simply no other way to convey one's status as a victim of the unfair allocation of society's resources. And unless you can show that you and your groups are more of a victim than the other guys and their groups, you *will* get the short end of the stick.

If this war were only a matter of property, it would be bad enough. But there is another dimension to it that is even more troubling. Government is not only stealing your property; it is stealing your mind. The game of whining for victim status requires you to *pretend* you don't see the illegitimacy of taking property from one to give it to another, and it requires you to *pretend* it doesn't bother you to have Government's non-discrimination regime co-opt your own moral obligation to discriminate among associations. All of this pretense is at the bottom of why we are becoming not just an amoral or an immoral nation, but a nation of moral zombies. It is the same phenomenon as what people call "political correctness," but it goes way beyond the stuff of late night talk shows and

Broadway plays. The fact is that you are required as a condition of playing the game, as a condition of being a relevant person in today's world, to accept Government's right to make moral judgements for you and to accept – or at least pretend that you don't reject – each and every one of Government's judgements. Most people who are good at the game get that way by internalizing these requirements. For them, which includes most people – especially the successful ones – not arguing about politically correct issues becomes second nature. But for some the hypocrisy and moral conflict just makes them crazy.

How is a white construction worker, shut out of a job by affirmative action, ever going to avoid blaming blacks and feeling racial animosity as a result? And how is a black man ever going to believe that white rage at affirmative action is anything but racism? How is either of them going to accept the other's rights, when each is schooled by the requirements of the war to think of himself as a victim of the other? Sound explosive? It is, but it gets worse. Even though each is induced to hate the other for not giving him more recognition of his victim status, neither is supposed to actually *feel* that hatred. If either assaults the other, he will be guilty not only of assault, but also of a hate crime, and subject to a harsher penalty. While most people would not act on any animosities they might feel, the situation is tailor made to incite those on the fringes to react violently. And it is tailor made to multiply both the number and anger of those on the fringes by politically parlaying any violence into further claims of victim status, greater amounts of retributive redistribution, and harsher hate crime penalties. Thus, Government's anti-discrimination "ethic" induces people to hate each other, then induces them to commit acts that make hatred justified, then fans the flames further in the hate crime hearings. Before you know it, those who may have harbored a little bit of residual racism have become fanatics, those few who had been fanatics before have multiplied like rabbits, and both David Duke and Al Sharpton have political careers.

All the while you are supposed to pretend that integration is your highest social goal and, if you don't, maybe submit to some sensitivity training at work. Nonetheless, it is a fact that even the majority who are not on the violent fringes tend to adopt their side's view of fairness (their "side" meaning their race), and to categorize people's probable attitudes according to the color of their skin. And this race-consciousness is *increasing*. What? Wasn't that kind of superficial categorization supposed to be what integration and desegregation were meant to prevent? Well, guess what? It is *increasing* in spite of our efforts at brainwashing people to ignore those politically incorrect attitudes that they actually have. In fact, the more we try to brainwash them to not have these attitudes, the more they seem to adopt them – and the more virulent they become. Our efforts to desegregate schools, for example, are a total washout. Not only are people re-segregating themselves, but it seems that the desegregation effort has made them *more* racist, not less. Researchers are finding that none, absolutely *none*, of Government's efforts to promote school integration has worked. In fact it seems now that any apparent success in that direction is being reversed in a re-segregation movement that has all the planners and pundits baffled. Even though surveys show that a majority of people from each race spout the party line preference for integrating, their actions don't show a willingness to actually do so.

All five guests on a News Hour with Jim Lehrer panel discussion (8/17/01) on re-segregation decried the phenomenon and called for greater efforts to attack it by doing something about people who are "segregated by income," as Sheryl Cashin from Georgetown University put it. This is the politically correct way to explain the failure of desegregation. Because there are income differentials, the thinking goes, people won't or can't integrate the way the policy wants them to. Well of course people are segregated by income. That is the point of doing well in life. Everyone wants to make more money primarily so that they can move out of the old neighborhood and up to a better one. But Cashin feels that segregation by income is "destabilizing" and leads to segregation by race. Among her utopian solutions is to make sure that "every child has a shot at a world class education." Like every liberal leveler who repeats this mantra, she emphasizes the word "every," as if their chanting could bring it about. And Gary Orfield, the Harvard researcher whose re-segregation study provided the grist for the evening's mill, argued strenuously for a renewed commitment to desegregation, with a particular focus on addressing the income inequalities that frustrate the policy.

Such sentiments are to be expected from liberals, of course, but the evening's token conservative, Ward Connerly, allowed as how he too was "terribly concerned about class inequities and income inequities." Connerly is the man known best for convincing California (where he is a member of the state university system's Board of Regents) to drop its affirmative action admission policies. That he apparently feels he must bow to the fairness god on the income question in order to maintain credibility for his conservative view on racial preferences is disturbing, but typical. As discussed in Chapter 1, all conservatives tend to set back their own cause by going with the liberal view in other areas. Thus, even in the doubtful event that California can hang onto its anti-affirmative action policies, the net effect is to hammer home more firmly that *inequalities should be addressed*. The end result again is that all debate on any issue that could involve Government's fairness role – regardless of who wins the debates – moves to more firmly establish that role. And the stronger that role gets, the more all people have to position themselves as victims. And the more they try to portray themselves as victims, the more that positioning requires them to hate those who might credibly be called their victimizers. What better way is there to prove you believe you have been victimized?

The polarizing effect of Government's fairness role, in which every word in every debate adds more fuel to the fire, is seen most clearly and chillingly in the lyrics of the songs that are attracting our youth. While the most violent and offensive of them are born on the fringes, the tendency is for everyone eventually to accept the fringe views as containing at least part-truths. It is important to realize that this is another one of those ugly positive feedback loops in operation. As long as Government is in the position of allocating outcomes, racism and other manifestations of the *war of all against all* will get worse and worse. There is no hope whatsoever that any bring-back-morality efforts, any censorship efforts, any pandering to the no-justice-no-peace chanters will ever produce a reduction in tensions. Nor will any adjustments to desegregation, integration or affirmative action policies. Every one of those efforts, as long as they continue to accept Government's redistributionist role, will only cause matters to worsen. And matters are clearly bad enough already. Here are some lyrics from rapper Ice T, followed by excerpts from an op-ed about a white power concert. The primary audience, in both cases, is young men and teenage boys.

> Squeeze the trigger.
> Cops hate kids, kids hate cops. Cops kill kid's with warnin' shots. What is crime and what is not? What is justice? I think I forgot. We buy weapons to keep us strong. Reagan sends guns where they don't belong. The controversy is thick and the drag is strong. But no matter the lies we all know who's wrong. Homeless sleep on the city streets. Waitin' to die with nothin' to eat, while rich politicians soak their feet in the pools at their ten million buck retreats. People hate people for color of face. No one had a choice in the race we were placed.
> Squeeze the trigger.

> "White power music is a growing phenomenon. Hammerfest 2000 didn't get a lot of news coverage, but it was the most successful white power concert in the U.S. last year. . . The two-day concert was a raging success for hard-core fans of Hitler and lynching and the developing ideology of 'pan-Aryanism.' A group called the Bully Boys drove the Nazi-saluting crowd into a frenzy with a song called 'Six Million More.' And all other references to the extermination of Jews and gays and the mass killing of blacks were warmly received. . .

The crowds at the concerts sing along, dance, hurl one another into mosh pits, salute swastikas and shout 'Heil Hitler'."[106]

It is clearly the default assumption of our policymakers that such outrageous views require more in the way of education, sensitivity training etc., as well as paying more attention to whatever the root causes of these kids' gripes might be. What I am suggesting is that such measures are largely responsible for the virulence of the problem we have today. Doing more of the same will only make things worse. As long as it is believed that Government will distribute "justice" (i.e., outcomes) fairly, it will be a good strategy for all groups – and for *every* child within each group – to fall into I-am-a-victim mode, and virulence. The only way to get these problems to recede is to remove Government from the role. While it might seem counterintuitive, not to mention frightening, to simply let race relations sort themselves out, that is the only thing that will work. On the current path it is anyone's guess whether our society will disintegrate first or explode.

Of course heightened racial tensions are not the only manifestation of the fight-for-your-slice war. Working women and gays are also becoming alienated from society precisely because of Government efforts to force everyone to include them. Here too the main method to enforce inclusion is brainwashing. This is the effect of all the anti-discrimination and harassment laws, the penalty boosters for "hate," and the sensitivity training for the recalcitrant. These measures work by marginalizing those who refuse to accept politically correct views. But in spite of such coercion to enforce inclusion, most people naturally remain resentful of the groups they are supposed to include, with the result that inclusion, like desegregation, is reversing. The traditionalists are resentful first of all because they disagree with these groups' sexual mores and attitudes toward work and family, and secondly because they disagree with giving them special rights to enforce their inclusion. But most of all they bridle at having to reprogram their own minds to incorporate these views with which they disagree. Others, of course, might call them backward and bigoted, and perhaps they are. But the fact remains that today you are not allowed to have certain opinions. Forget the First Amendment. Forget any rights you thought you had. If you want to have a job and a career, you will be required to expunge any such thoughts from your mind lest they slip out in front of your boss or your co-workers. The speech police are out in force, as are the thought police looking for bad attitudes.

While many people's moral choices would coincide with those of Government, in a diverse, morally vibrant society it is certain that some would not. Therefore the requirement of everyone to enforce politically correct unanimity is

---

[106] The New York Times op-ed by Bob Herbert, "High-Decibel Hate," August 20, 2001.

bound to require everyone to participate in coercion. This is, in itself, immoral. It is the "gleichschaltung" of Nazi Germany, and it amounts to the usurpation by Government of every individual's power to decide for himself what is moral. Most unconscionably, *gleichschaltung* forces everyone *as a matter of moral obligation* to participate in the coercion. In fact, though, it amounts to a direct violation of the first words of the First Amendment in the Bill of Rights: "Congress shall make no law respecting an establishment of religion, or prohibiting the free exercise thereof." The religion Congress has established is that which requires the universal belief that the greatest moral good is the right of our politicians to keep themselves in power by deciding what is good for us.

Constitutional Government

So bound up are our pols today in competing to do good things for us that they cannot any longer imagine that that is not what we want, or what we meant when we said, "That to secure these Rights [to 'Life, Liberty and the Pursuit of Happiness'] Governments were instituted among Men, deriving their just Powers from the Consent of the Governed." Our rights are what the philosophers call "negative" values, which, boiled down, means that we want to be left alone to pursue our own interests, as opposed to having anyone take positive actions to help us. It has long been recognized that political consensus is far easier on negative rights like ours than on positive rights to get Government or other citizens to give us things. In fact if you think about it – which our Founders did – you can see that having positive rights is a formula for disintegration, because it eventually will be impossible to achieve consensus on who gets what and who pays for it. That is why Government in America was instituted to make sure that each citizen had rights to his own protected space, not to be unreasonably encroached upon by other citizens or Government. At least that is the way it was supposed to be, and it worked for a while. But it is incompatible with the task of protecting our original rights for politicians to be taking property from one citizen to give it to another, *even if* a greater good will result from the transfer. Today, of course, that's all they do. So locked in to the do-gooder mentality are our politicians that they have long since lost any concept that their powers were to be "limited" or "enumerated," to pick the two words that nostalgic or naïve constitutionalists at the libertarian think tanks like to remind us of.

How and why did we get off track? Perhaps we were led astray by the few explicit errors the Founders made in providing for Government roles that were incompatible with the Constitution's overriding philosophy. Examples might include the Article I, Section 8 authorizations of Congress "To establish Post Offices and post Roads" and "To promote the Progress of Science and useful Arts, by securing for limited times to Authors and Inventors the exclusive Right to their Writings and Discoveries." Or perhaps, by positively enumerating the Bill of Rights, we diluted our general negative-value rights to life, liberty and the pursuit of happiness. The Founders were apparently worried about this, which is why they included the Ninth Amendment admonition that "The enumeration in the Constitution of certain rights shall not be construed to deny or disparage others retained by the people." But the Ninth Amendment has clearly been ignored. The First Amendment's right to "freedom of speech," for example, originally intended as a protection against suppression of political dissent, has been used to justify all manner of egalitarian claims to the property of others, even a right to sunbathe on a private beach in Greenwich, Connecticut. Or perhaps *separation of powers* was not as good an idea as the Founders thought it was. It certainly hasn't prevented the use of the Constitution itself as a principal tool of the courts to effect the disintegration of its original values.

Regardless of where the problem came from, its most frightening feature now is that many prominent figures have written eloquently and forcefully about it, but it keeps on getting worse. To see if we can understand why, let's look at several analyses by thoughtful people, and what they would suggest as remedies. Hayek put the problem this way:

> "[T]he possession of unlimited power makes it impossible for a representative body to make the general principles prevail on which all agree, because under such a system the majority of the representative assembly, in order to remain a majority, *must* do what it can to buy the support of the several interests by granting them special benefits. . . It appears that we have unwittingly created a machinery which makes it possible to claim the sanction of an alleged majority for measures which are in fact not desired by a majority, and which may even be disapproved by a majority of the people; and that this machinery produces an aggregate of measures that not only is not wanted by anybody, but that could not as a whole be approved by any rational mind because it is inherently contradictory." [Original emphasis.][107]

Thus, while Hayek admired democracy as the only form of Government yet devised that can accomplish the peaceful transfer of power, he warned at length of the dangers of *unrestrained* democracy, which is what he believed America developed in the twentieth century, in spite of its separation of powers. The Legislative and Executive branches, of course, are meant to check any abuses by each other. And, as we all learned in school, the Judicial Branch is there to iron out any disputes, and will be guided by the Constitution in doing so. It was a reasonable idea and, according to Hayek, worked for some time. But eventually, the lure of unlimited power caused any restraints that may have worked to break down, leading all three branches to be more cooperative with than restraining of each others' abuses. The inescapable conclusion is that the separation of powers concept, or how it was set up, did not work.

As remedy, Hayek offers a new Model Constitution, of which he humbly disclaims any intent to recommend that it should be used to replace the constitution of any real nation, such as the United States. Nonetheless, he sounds serious

---

[107] Friedrich A. Hayek, *Law, Legislation and Liberty*, Vol. 3, *The Political Order of a Free People*, 1979.

enough, and has a very detailed blueprint, right down to the terms, ages, and election methods for the proposed new Government's officials. His model would create two separate bodies. A Legislative Assembly would determine " the rules of just conduct" that everyone has to abide by, while a Governmental Assembly would administer the necessary functions of Government according to those rules. Finally, a Constitutional Court would act as a "court of last instance" to resolve any "conflict of competence between the two assemblies [which might arise] through the questioning by one of the validity of the resolution passed by the other."[108]

I have no doubt that Hayek's plan would be an improvement on what we have today, provided that his methods of keeping the Legislative Assembly on task would work. Nonetheless, I think he was unfortunately right that it could not serve as a realistic plan that any country could switch to. Among the difficulties in the United States would be that, although on the surface it looks something like the three-way separation between our Executive, Legislative and Judicial branches, it would in practice require a wholesale replacement of them all. This is not just an amendment. This is a whole new constitution. Even if all the details could be worked out, it is still not clear to me how the Legislative Assembly would get working on the rules of just conduct, or what the first ones would be. Which leads to my even bigger concern with Hayek's plan: It would be difficult or impossible to gain public understanding of what the problem is, why this major structural overhaul might cure it, and what benefits we could expect and when. Without such understanding, it would be impossible to amass political support for its implementation

Another clear thinker on these issues and, by no coincidence, an Austrian School adherent like Hayek, was Bruno Leoni. Hayek considered Leoni's approach brilliant, but impractical, perhaps because he died suddenly in 1967 before he was able to fully articulate it. Nonetheless, it has to me a certain revolutionary appeal. He begins with the Golden Rule, or, more properly, the negative value version of it.

> "A very old principle appears to have been violated in contemporary society – a principle already enunciated in the Gospel and, much earlier, in the Confucian philosophy: 'Do not do unto others what you would not wish others to do unto you.' I do not know of any other statement in the modern philosophy of freedom that sounds so strikingly concise as this. It may seem dull in comparison with the sophisticated formulae sometimes clothed in obscure mathematical

---

[108] Friedrich A. Hayek, *Law, Legislation and Liberty*, Vol. 3, *The Political Order of a Free People*, 1979.

symbols that people seem to like so much today in economics as well as in political science. Nevertheless, the Confucian principle would appear to be still applicable for the restoration and the preservation of individual freedom at the present time."[109]

Leoni, a practicing lawyer in Italy and fluent not only in the languages but in the English, French, German and Italian legal traditions and their ancient antecedents, thought the Golden Rule could re-emerge through an effective return of the common law. This would be brought about by increasing acceptance of the notion that legislation would have to pass through a Golden Rule filter to be considered valid. Leoni believed that legislation, as opposed to the common law that everyone accepts (similar to Hayek's *rules of just conduct*), was ephemeral, biased toward the ends of interest groups, and bound to violate freedom eventually. He thought people should reject legislation if it required "constraining any other people to do what they would never do without the constraint." And Leoni didn't just mean we should reject legislation before it passed. He meant that, if it didn't measure up, we should collectively ignore it. Leoni had his fingers crossed that when legislation conflicted with a mutual sense of just conduct between parties, those parties might simply ignore legislated law in favor of their contracts and common law treatments of property. Although he provides a few examples of earlier reversions to the common law, he would probably recognize some examples developing today in such phenomena as the sagebrush rebellions in the American West and the backlashes against affirmative action.

While I think there is some hope for the reversion to common law that Leoni optimistically envisioned, I suspect the more likely scenario is that any steps in that direction will be overwhelmed by the positive feedback loop driving us in the opposite direction, i.e., toward full socialism. It seems unrealistic to expect piecemeal displeasure with various legislative measures to provide a foundation for the return of freedom in any of the countries whose constitutions or traditions were not able to keep it there in the first place. I would note, however, that both Leoni's and Hayek's focus on the Golden Rule[110] could eventually provide a philosophical basis for a truly understandable and, therefore, politically viable plan of action.

---

[109] Bruno Leoni, *Freedom and the Law*, 1991, from lectures delivered in 1958.

[110] Hayek's Model Constitution would provide Golden Rule-like protection as follows: "the individual can be restrained only in such conduct as may encroach upon the protected domain of others, [and] he would under such a provision be wholly unrestricted in all actions which affected only his personal domain or that of other consenting responsible persons, and thus be assured of all freedom that can be secured by political action." Hayek makes the point that such a provision would render any list of specific rights, such as the Rights of Man or the Bill of Rights, entirely redundant and unnecessary. Friedrich A. Hayek, *Law, Legislation and Liberty*, Vol. 3, *The Political Order of a Free People*, 1979.

In his 1996 book, *Slouching Towards Gomorrah*, Robert Bork makes a clear and compelling case that the courts, and particularly the Supreme Court, are to blame for abandoning the Constitution in service of an activist liberal agenda. His is a particularly cautionary tale for anyone who might naively rely on any written words, such as in a Constitution, to provide meaningful and permanent protections for freedom, because it is clear from Bork that the courts can use those very words to undermine their own intent. He also notes that in earlier days, when the fashion was to leave the Constitution behind in service of *conservative* activism, Judge Learned Hand suggested repeal of the due process clauses of the Fifth and Fourteenth Amendments, since these were the passages through which activists inserted their "judicial legislation."

Bork characterized Hand's proposal as "extreme," perhaps to make his own seem a little less so. Moreover, he implies that it wouldn't by itself work, anyway, because other means would later be discovered to accomplish activist ends, such as the equal protection clause. So, rather than impossibly chasing our tail by repealing every new phrase the courts start abusing, Bork would put political restraints on the courts, including especially the Supreme Court. Bork's amendment would "make any federal or state court decision subject to being overturned by a majority vote of each House of Congress." While I agree with Bork's analysis of the problem of liberal judicial activism, and I believe his proposed amendment would be beneficial in retarding it, I have two problems with it. First, getting it passed and ratified would suffer from all the problems of Hayek's Model Constitution in terms of mustering the public understanding of and support for its purposes, and would be just as nebulous and uncertain as to if and when it would do any good with regard to those purposes. Secondly, as Bork clearly articulated in 1978 in *The Antitrust Paradox*, antitrust law is valid and constitutional as law. And, for all my disagreements with him on the economics of antitrust, I see no reason to doubt his legal and constitutional analysis. Therefore, I would not expect the Bork approach to solve my main problem, however much good it might do elsewhere.

William Niskanen offers some intriguing insights into the nature and source of the problem. Like Bork, he sees the courts as having fumbled their role: "Judicial review has not been sufficient to prevent a massive erosion of the limits on the powers of the federal government." [111] He points out that, although the Constitution did not contain any provision for resolving disputes, early on the Supreme Court stepped into the role, which Chief Justice John Marshall thought was implied in a Constitution intended to limit the powers of Government. But, in spite of having used the implied limiting function of the Constitution as their authorization for the role, the courts have limited neither the expansion of the other

---

[111] William A. Niskanen, "On the Constitution of a Compound Republic," Cato Institute, 2001. Niskanen is chairman of the Cato Institute and is a former acting chairman of President Reagan's Council of Economic Advisers.

branches, nor their own, demonstrating that "political power rushes to fill a vacuum." Niskanen's solution is another form of the separation of powers, in this case envisioning a means by which federal and state Governments would check each other's abuses of power. His analysis is particularly interesting because he finds traces of his remedies in unused or poorly applied provisions already in the Constitution. The federal Government, in Niskanen's plan, would check the states' abuses by reasserting "its authority to protect the privileges and immunities of individuals against unjust state actions, so that the rights of individuals are not dependent on the weaker procedural guarantees of due process and equal protection." The states would check federal abuses by allowing a vote by a certain number of them to nullify an unjust action and, perhaps, by allowing states to secede. Needless to say, every aspect of Niskanen's plan would be highly contentious and, like the other plans mentioned – with the possible exception of Leoni's – be difficult for the public to understand and, therefore, hard to gather political support for. And, like all the others, because its effects would be distant and uncertain, it is unclear if, how and when its implementation would begin to rein in confiscation or affect the antitrust laws. The nebulous nature of the results of such plans would, in the end, make it very difficult or impossible to gather political support for them.

All of the approaches mentioned recognize that the Constitution we have now has somehow failed to produce the limiting effect our Founders had in mind. And this was not a minor error: This is why they wrote it down. So all of these modern redrafters take our Founders' separation of powers in different directions, repairing and shoring up the loopholes or omissions that kept separation from doing its job. I have no doubt that all these proposals would be improvements on what we have today. I also have no doubt that our society no longer has the energy and attention span to contemplate starting over. Largely because we have lost control of Government, the only initiatives that can get up a head of steam politically are those that have tangible and relatively immediate expected benefits, that is to say, those that are based on the presumed correctness of Government's redistributionist role. The political questions of the day are all of the "What have you done for me lately" variety, or "What can you do for me today." Nobody has the time for philosophical discursions into the nature and structure of Government. These are the kinds of measures that only a newly forming nation would have the energy to address and implement. It is hard to imagine a country that thinks it's got it all figured out taking on such wholesale changes, especially when they would take it in the opposite direction. Nonetheless, this is what needs to be done. The question is: Is there a more direct and easily understood way to do it? I think there may be.

The Rule of Law Amendment

My approach would leave the structure we have today, but explicitly limit Government confiscation or any other reshuffling of the property or prospects of the people. I believe this is roughly what the Founders had in mind with "Pursuit of Happiness." In any case, I believe it would repair in one fell swoop all the holes in our constitutional dike that socialism is flooding through. While the proposal would have a radical effect across the board, and be opposed by many with an interest in Government, it would also be relatively easy to understand. I would hope, therefore, that it could also develop support across the board from all those interested in Liberty. Specifically, I would propose the following amendment to the Constitution:

The Rule of Law Amendment
No law in these United States of America may alter the relative economic or social standing of U.S. citizens. Laws related to defense and policing powers are exempt from this article. [112]

I would suggest calling it the Rule of Law Amendment, because I believe it would have the effect of banishing all of the most arbitrary violations of that principle inherent in today's vote-buying, rent-seeking, influence-peddling America. Alternative names might include the Equal Treatment Amendment or the No Special Rights Amendment. Wags in favor of it might call it the Anti Alphabet Soup Amendment or the Get Off My Back Amendment. Those opposed may settle on the Unfairness Amendment, since it will prohibit all Government efforts to redress inequalities or provide assistance, such as affirmative action, progressive income taxes, Welfare, Medicaid, Medicare, Social Security, public housing and public schools. It would also ban Government-blessed steel cartels, Government-set milk price supports, and Government-organized prescription drug buying cartels. It would nix the minimum wage and the Davis Bacon Act's requirement to pay the "prevailing wage" on Government construction jobs. Trade would truly be free, because the Government would not be allowed to interfere in setting any import or export quotas, tariffs or other preferences or penalties.

---

[112] Not being a lawyer, much less a constitutional scholar, I may have gone overboard in my attempt to be brief. For example, I have assumed that what is meant by the word "law" is either already understood, or can be made so by external explanations of intent. If not, more detailed descriptions can be used. In any case, what I mean by "law" is law, rule or policy enacted or administered by any elected, appointed or otherwise duly constituted authority of any Federal, State, County, or Municipal Government or delegated agents thereof, including all departments, agencies, commissions and similar bodies. Similarly, what I mean by "alter" is have the intended, expected or actual effect of altering.

It would allow the taking of private property for public purposes, but only if the purpose is sufficiently general that all could be deemed to benefit, and only if the purpose could not and would not be served by private entities (since this would effectively alter the status of citizens involved with those entities). Moreover, takings for public purposes would only be allowed if the owner is sufficiently compensated so that his economic or social standing is not altered. Environmental rules that are effective takings could be enacted, but, again, only if the environmental benefit is sufficiently general, and only if the owner is sufficiently compensated so as not to alter his relative economic or social standing. The Post Office would go, as would the Patent Office. The one being a large Government monopoly, and the other being charged with doling out Government monopolies, both cause major and ongoing alterations in the economic and social standing of U.S. citizens. And both functions can readily be replaced by private entities (such as UPS or Federal Express, and the privately won network monopolies that actually have value to consumers rather than to lawyers and bureaucrats).

There would be no FCC, FTC, Department of Commerce or Department of Energy, except to the degree their activities involve policing functions, such as for fraud. Ditto for the SEC, which has both a legitimate policing function and an illegitimate market design function, which regularly creates or destroys businesses and thereby has an ongoing effect on the relative economic or social standing of citizens. The Department of Justice would drop its Antitrust Division, which, like the SEC's National Market System, has major status-altering effects on U.S. citizens, and stick to administering the courts and legitimate policing functions, such as the FBI. Similarly, the FDA would focus on making sure food and drugs are safe, a policing function, and drop worrying about whether they are effective. (All drugs now must be proven to be both "safe *and* effective" before they are approved.) Drug companies would be free to conduct any tests of their choosing to determine effectiveness, provided participants were informed of the nature and risks of the tests. They would also be free to market unproved drugs, provided they did not fail to inform buyers of pertinent known facts, or lack thereof, regarding the expected efficacy and/or dangers of taking the drugs. The FDA and perhaps other policing agencies, such as the FBI, would protect citizens from harm due to fraudulent claims (which is theft) or physical violence due to undisclosed but known dangers from bad food or drugs.

Justice would be required to be blind; it would not be allowed to discriminate. There would be no special laws protecting particular groups of people and no hate crime laws. Laws to redress past grievances or to forcibly "level the playing field" would be banned, because they alter the status of individuals and groups. Laws that protect everyone against assault, murder, fraud, theft, impersonation or other forms of violence to person or property, being general, would not be affected by the Amendment.

Note that the Rule of Law Amendment would prohibit *Government* policies that alter status. It would leave alone any private efforts to adopt such policies, neither discouraging nor encouraging them. This would allow the natural organization of economic and social life. Cartels would be OK, as would consumer boycotts, direct or secondary. Union organizing would be fine, as would firing union organizers. People and groups would be allowed to associate or refrain from associating with whomever they want, for any reason. Owners of buildings and businesses would be free to rent to or hire anyone they want, or refuse to do so for any reason. While they would be free to not rent to or hire women or minorities, so would corporations and consumers be free to organize groups that buy only from all-women or all-minority firms, or only from firms with affirmative action programs. They could also organize boycotts of businesses that arbitrarily discriminate. Restaurants would be free to allow or disallow anyone on their premises, and diners and businesses would be free to organize boycotts of any restaurant for any reason. There would be no Government funding of education or science, and no auctions of spectrum. There would be no Government-administered affirmative action or other preferences in hiring, promotion, admission, or contracting. Private educational or scientific institutions (and there would no longer be any other kind) would be free to adopt any preferential programs they choose.

Civil rights advocates may expect setbacks from these changes. But I don't think that is how it would turn out. In the first place, the Rule of Law Amendment would outlaw any Government discrimination, such as in policies that deny voting rights to anyone, or try to gerrymander voting districts to neutralize or disenfranchise certain groups of voters. And it would require blind administration of such Government matters as trials and penalties for crimes. Blind, that is, to race, sex, national origin, religion, sexual preference etc. – the list is infinitely long because it includes all persons. In the second place, any dispassionate observer of the application of preferential policies by Government is himself blind if he cannot see that such policies have become the chief cause today of the ugly kinds of discrimination that hold minorities back. They contribute to the presumption that minority and women applicants are less likely to be qualified for the positions they are seeking, for example, and are more likely to cause huge legal headaches if hired. Moreover, the "rainbow coalition" is splintering as the *war of all against all* heats up. Blacks, for example, might reasonably resent the inclusion of gays as deserving of the same preferences they get, both because most of them consider non-heterosexuals immoral, and because they know that potential employers do, too. This means that employers are likely to put them both in the same preferential pot – i.e., as preferred *not-hires* if they can possibly get away with it. And women must know by now that one reason they are not advancing even *to* the glass ceiling anymore is the danger employers face from discrimination and sexual harassment suits. Worst of all, by forcing all of these groups to compete for preferenced positions, they are all bound to become jealous, suspicious, resentful and even hateful of each other. The result is an increasing unwillingness to deal with people on merit, and a virtual requirement to see them for their surface qualities – race, sex, national origin etc. If that's not discrimination, what is it? The bottom line is that the Rule of Law Amendment would allow the natural progress of minorities to resume, and racism – which had been on the decline until affirmative action came around – to again recede.

Taxes could be raised to fund the legitimate defense, policing and other functions of Government, provided such functions are either exempt, such as defense and policing, or are sufficiently general as to be non-altering of the economic or social status of citizens. The method of taxation would also have to be general and non-altering. Income taxes would probably pass muster, as would sales or consumption taxes. Taxing different citizens at different rates, however, would not. Nor would loopholes, credits, exemptions, or other preferences for any purpose. Anyone nostalgic over the loss of all those fun and games at 1040 time can console himself with the thought that Government would cost so much less that taxes would drop drastically. The flat taxes of Steve Forbes and others have been projecting "revenue neutral" rates (i.e., rates that would raise the same amounts as the current progressive system, perhaps dynamically adjusted a little for presumed stronger growth) of 17 or 18% with an exemption for the first $30,000 or $35,000. My guess is that the Rule of Law Amendment would cut the cost of discretionary Government spending by 90% and enable a flat tax rate of 5%, even with generous defense and policing budgets, and fully covering non-discretionary items like interest on the debt. And speaking of the debt, that would quickly melt away and never come back, because the growth released by removing the dysfunctional intrusions of Government would likely raise far more revenues than imagined, even at 5% or less. State and city costs of Government – and intrusions – would come down drastically too, causing their tax rates to crash as well. In the end it may be possible to fund all levels of legitimate Government at 5% or less of our income or consumption.

The transition to a Rule of Law America would take time, although some effects would be immediate. The issuing of new patents and copyrights would cease, for example, as would antitrust enforcement. In contrast, existing patents or previously arranged property distributions under the settlement terms of past enforcement actions would probably remain until scheduled expiration, if any. For most patents that would be 17 years from issuance. All obligations of the

Government that have been actually or implicitly incurred, such as to all the reasonably imminent retirees expecting Social Security, including those over, say, 50 years of age, would be honored. Similarly, in the degree to which people have adjusted their financial arrangements in anticipation of current or reasonably imminent future benefits, those benefits would be paid (although it may be tricky determining how much and for how long). For Government employees who would become redundant, it would be appropriate to provide some level of transitional financial assistance, as well perhaps as job training and placement help.

October 4, 2001

Afterward

In the three weeks since the World Trade Center attack, Americans have struggled to understand why so many Muslims hate us. The most common answer is that they hate us because they hate freedom. This could not be and is not true. Political freedom, the right of a people to determine their own destiny, is both the most fundamental thing we Americans mean by freedom, and what those angry Muslims are now fighting us to get. They see a hypocritical America preaching democracy while propping up one unpopular regime after another in *their* homeland, most of which would be toppled if elections were held. Since we are the Beacon of Liberty that led the Western World to economic prosperity, we just cannot imagine that anyone – especially poor Muslims – wouldn't want what we are ramming down their throats. Given our own history, we should know better.

The instant outpouring of worldwide sympathy for America, Americans and others from over 60 countries [113] lost in the September 11th attacks has led many to hope that a new global coalition will form to defeat terrorism, or at least hold it at bay. Unfortunately, this war-on-terrorism formulation fundamentally misconstrues the main problem. These are not Basque separatists or the Irish Republican Army. Fighting them *would* require the combination of police, military, intelligence and international cooperation assets that President Bush is assembling. But what we face now are increasingly powerful acts of war by many primarily Muslim countries that – wittingly or unwittingly – sponsor anti-*American* terror in their shadows. The most important weapon for this war is a fierce adherence to the principles of freedom. As this book has described, America is far from perfect in this regard, in spite of its reputation and its historical and rhetorical attachment to the concept. We must be very careful that our efforts to assemble allies do not reflect the socialist priorities that have come to dominate domestic policies. If they do, we will both undermine our own ability to fight and increase the size and strength of the enemy.

The requirements of coalition-building – rewarding friendly regimes and punishing unfriendly ones – are largely responsible for the virulent Muslim

---

[113] New York Mayor Rudolph Giuliani put the number of countries who lost citizens in the World Trade Center at 63 on Larry King Live, October 3, 2001. On October 4 the Wall Street Journal article, "In Attack on Terrorism, U.S. Has Early Priority: Managing Its Message," refers to a State Department Web site that pinpoints the location of 81 countries who lost citizens in all the attacks of September 11th.

extremism we now confront, and especially for its rapid coalescing of otherwise diverse factions around a unified hate-America stance. I should be clear that I am not talking about mutual defense alliances, which are appropriate and can be effective both to fight terrorism and to wage war. But we will run into big problems if we seek to hold any coalition together by dispensing aid, trade agreements, debt relief or other differential treatments of the parties to the coalition, especially if such policies are meant to be pursued on a long term and continuing basis. This, of course, is exactly what we are doing now. As a result, we will find that the policy we are pursuing to contain terrorism is essentially an intensification of that which created the current threat, and will make matters worse.

To understand why this is so it is necessary to recognize that America's engagement in world affairs is characterized by the same interventionism that is causing so much trouble at home – i.e., by those disastrous redistributionist policies discussed extensively in this book. Just as our professional politicians and other elements of the policy elite are always busy allocating outcomes to promote "fairness" domestically, the same policies are applied globally to achieve "fairness" everywhere, often by the same people. And, just as the Government Fairness Enterprise here fosters the dissension, whining, victimizing, victims and hatred of the *war of all against all*, the same principles applied internationally also foster vehement claims of victimization, angry demands for "justice" – and terrorism. Moreover, because abroad we are always wading into situations that are none of our business, we immediately become the target of the ethnic, religious or other historical grievances of any previously warring factions. Indeed, our presence causes the local parties to ratchet up any conflicts that already existed, and to create conflicts that weren't there before. Why? Because, as we saw in the last chapter, attacking rivals – verbally or physically – and complaining of bias by policymakers constitute wise strategy for any party to our ministrations, whether we are allocating economic outcomes at home or distributing aid, trade agreements, sanctions and "peace" abroad. From the time we set ourselves (or the UN) up as arbiter, it becomes good strategy for the antagonists to claim victim status and to back up the claim by angrily demonstrating against and attacking their alleged victimizers. In other words, terrorism becomes a good strategy. This is the international equivalent of the racial animosity and increasingly frequent atrocities provoked by such policies as affirmative action and hate crime laws here at home.

But it is much worse abroad. Even genocide is a good political strategy if your people are to be forced by the UN or US to live in a multi-ethnic or multi-religious democracy with your enemies. It is astounding to me that policymakers have ignored the obvious correlation between their peace processes around the world and ethnic cleansing. Whether we're on the way in, as in Kosovo during the bombing strikes against Serbian forces in 1999, [114] or on the way out, as in Rwanda in 1994, [115] the very presence or threat of a peace process imposed by the UN or US gives powerful incentives for the parties to kill off rival populations as quickly as possible whenever the peacekeepers aren't looking or can't stop it. Given the difficulties described in the last chapter that even we in America have had keeping our own democracy on a constitutional track, it should hardly be surprising that sworn historical enemies would initiate genocide at the prospect of any superpower-imposed (or UN-imposed) democracy. Why *not* kill your rivals before they can simply vote away your rights and property?

America and the endless tangle of world agencies it dominates are constantly engaged in applying aid here and sanctions there, redrawing borders here and demanding democracy there, moving US or UN troops this way and that, into and out of the Somalias, Bosnias, Rwandas and Lebanons. And the sad string of useless accords – Dayton, Paris, Camp David, Oslo etc. – leave poignant reminders of the hopes for peace dashed by the realities of the "peace process." These interventions have produced no friends we did not already have, and have caused our enemies to proliferate. If you think about it, this result is inevitable. By aiding a friendly regime that is strong enough or democratically electable on its own, we have not gained anything we would not have had anyway. But by propping up weak or unelectable regimes, we are bound to anger either majorities disenfranchised by our maneuvers or disappointed dictators who would have been strong enough to dominate their populations – or both. In any case we are preventing a natural outcome that cannot but leave strong resentment of our intrusions by those most able to mount threats to them. We claim justification for these interventions on moral grounds, of course. We say we are on "humanitarian" missions to prevent famine, refugee crises, oppression, human rights abuses, genocide and other war

---

[114] From a U.S. Department of State report, "Erasing History: Ethnic Cleansing in Kosovo," May, 1999:

"MARCH 24. Beginning on or shortly after the commencement of the NATO airstrikes, VJ forces reportedly joined police and paramilitary units in systematically expelling ethnic Albanians from both villages and larger towns. Population centers that had not been targeted before and had no KLA presence were now being emptied. Thousands of dwellings reportedly were looted and torched. Serbian forces allegedly significantly accelerated their large-scale confiscation and destruction of documents. Reports of atrocities increased significantly.

MARCH 29. By this time there were reports that the majority of the 1.6 million ethnic Albanians in Kosovo may have been displaced from their homes. Whole towns and villages had been emptied. UNHCR reports estimated that Serbian forces had forcibly expelled upwards of 70,000 persons into Albania over the weekend. Refugees reported the forced separation of military-aged men from groups, summary executions in at least 20 towns and villages, and the widespread looting and burning of homes."

[115] The Atlantic Monthly magazine article by Samantha Power, "Bystanders to Genocide," September 2001. The article makes clear that the one time the UN and US could have made a positive contribution to the prevention of genocide, our feckless politicians flubbed it. So anxious were they to avoid a repeat of the Somalia debacle, that they pulled well armed UN troops *out* of Rwanda just as it became obvious that mass genocide by machete was about to occur. Led by the Clinton administration, the UN members on the ground gave political cover for each other and their retreating coalition by refusing to acknowledge that genocide was occurring, even though they clearly knew that it was.

crimes. But the United States Government is not a private relief agency. Our help always comes with quid pro quos and strings attached that inevitably anger more people than we help. And any dispassionate observer would conclude that, for all our pious proclamations, the results have almost always been the opposite of what we intended. Our policies are actually *causing* or *accelerating* the abuses we seek to prevent, such as genocide, even as our confused policymakers mutter "never again" in reference to the Holocaust. [116]

Worse, playing this game when there are multiple disenfranchised majorities or disappointed dictators all in the same region and sharing a common religion is potentially fatal to America. Not only are we actually causing the humanitarian disasters we seek to prevent, but our intervening and coalition building to that end is forcing the unification of diverse Muslim populations, sects and ethnicities around a common enemy: America. While it may still be true that most Muslims are not anti-American, we could not adopt a better policy to tip them over to the other side than the global us-against-them coalition against terror that we are now building. I know we are trying to make clear that it is terrorists, not Muslims, that we are going after. And I am aware that we are trying to drop wheat on the refugees that our war is starving to prove the point. But such policies have always backfired before and they are bound to backfire now. [117] Whether we are talking about soldiers in Pakistan's army, [118] or students in Indonesia [119] or, for that matter, in America, almost every Muslim community has some that sympathize with the radical view. The best way to tip the balance of opinion in their favor is for America to lead a global coalition against Muslim terror, especially one endorsed

---

[116] The Atlantic Monthly magazine article by Samantha Power, "Bystanders to Genocide," September 2001.

[117] MSNBC was already reporting concerns on September 29, 2001 that food intended for Afghan refugees would feed Taliban soldiers, not refugees. Similarly, it has long been clear that little of the medical and other humanitarian assistance intended for the people of Iraq has made it to its intended recipients, but has been shortstopped by Saddam's legions. And US economic sanctions have hurt only the people of Iraq, not Saddam, while providing him with great material for propaganda to recruit Muslims worldwide to his cause.

[118] Newsweek Magazine article, "A Dictator's Dilemma," October 1, 2001. "By now, experts estimate that 30 percent of the officers [in Pakistan's army] consider themselves fundamentalist Muslims." "If large-scale rioting were to break out in Pakistan as a result of U.S. strikes against Afghanistan, the Army might start to totter. That conjures up some scary possibilities. For one thing, imagine what bin Laden and his friends could do with Pakistan's small but lethal arsenal of nuclear weapons." Also see the New York Times article, "U.S. and Pakistan Discuss Nuclear Security," October 1, 2001. "The focus of the discussions last week was on how to protect weapons and create a new layer of restrictions on personnel handling them. The fear is that if there is a sustained Western attack on Afghanistan, unrest could boil over in Pakistan. Those strains would be reflected in the Pakistan Army, experts say, and there is a threat that Afghan-sympathizers in the military might seize control of nuclear weapons in Pakistan."

[119] The New York Times article, "Indonesia Radicals Issue Threats of Holy War," September 29, 2001. "'As human beings, we are very, very sad about the deaths at the World Trade Center,' said Mr. Siregar [who is said to have met Osama bin Laden]. 'But we must take the analysis farther. What happened was the result of American policy that oppresses Muslims. This shows that arrogance will be punished wherever it is. Now America is confused, panicked, broken inside.' Muhammad Naufal Dunggio, a researcher at an Islamic university who leads an allied radical group said he, too, had studied in the United States and had not liked it. 'I lived in Virginia' he said as recruits listened, 'and I'm telling you, the American people, they do not like Muslims.' "

at our insistence by the UN. No matter how we pretend that it's not just Muslim terrorists that we are going after (as if we would target those Basque separatists or the IRA), and no matter how we try to spin the effort as not an American but a world campaign ("terror can happen to anyone," "it's an attack on freedom everywhere," "it's an attack on civilization itself") it will be 100% clear to any Muslims considering the radical view that it is really only Muslim terrorists we are after, and that America is the leader of the coalition chasing them.

The fact is that it is not possible to give the impression that we are going after *all* terrorism, because we aren't, nor should we. In *this* war, it is only *Muslim* terror that poses the potentially mortal threat to America. And it is also a fact that, while other capitalist countries present targets besides those that are explicitly American, the ones that pose a danger to *us* now – and to Western Capitalism – are dangerous because they are *American* targets. Targets such as American embassies, businesses and other symbols of our presence in the world, including the businesses and embassies of our allies and trading partners, are attractive to the Muslim terrorists only in the degree to which they indirectly get at America. And now that terrorism has exploded onto our shores, those indirect means of attacking America have receded in relative attractiveness in the enemy's eyes, especially now that his suicide fanatics are clearly living amongst us. Therefore, it is not necessary or appropriate to include all the other countries in our coalition. Doing so only hampers our flexibility to respond in our own defense, and generates animosity toward the United States in the Muslim world.

While the Bush administration was very pleased when the UN on September 28 acceded to our request to require all of its 189 member states to cooperate with our war on terror, it is hard to imagine a more dangerous political development for our country. The headline alone probably produced thousands of terrorist recruits. And when has the UN ever demonstrated the power to compel more than rhetorical compliance in such a venture? Worse, by formalizing the coalition approach, we have only locked ourselves in to constraints on the use of our own power to defend ourselves. Only days after the resolution mandating cooperation against terror passed, UN Secretary General Kofi Annan was already clarifying it by explaining that it did not authorize changing regimes or moving militarily on any countries that may support terror without certified proof, presumably proof that would satisfy all the 189 legal systems of the UN's constituent members. It will undoubtedly require a lot of wheeling and dealing on trade, aid, etc to get and keep all those members on our side. In fact, since their interests often conflict in very fundamental ways, this is an impossible task.

All of this international interventionism and coalition building, like its counterpart, domestic socialism, is fraught with unintended consequences. There is not now and never has been any evidence that the international planners are any better at fashioning social arrangements than the domestic ones. While our best and brightest may have the degrees and experience to convince us that they can master all the flows of economic, ethnic, religious, political and other ingredients in the stew of human engagement to keep us on the right side of developments, or shape them favorably for us, they can't now and never could. But the difference between the socialist doodlers in our domestic economy, such as the antitrust agencies, and their foreign policy counterparts is that the latter are playing with live ammunition. The best current example of the unintended consequences of foreign intervention is in Afghanistan. Somehow the "freedom fighters" we once trained and armed to resist the Soviets have themselves become the trainers of the militant Islamic fundamentalists from around the world who now oppose America – and they've still got our stingers!

With 20/20 hindsight we can see at least some of the failures of policy, intelligence, vision and attention span that produced this disaster. But it is unlikely that we have learned enough from our mistakes to refashion the situation favorably this time. And it is certain that we have not learned that it is our meddling and intrusive planning for these faraway peoples that is the problem in the first place. Just as the domestic planners are always ready with more planning to address the messes they have caused, the foreign policy experts are now full of new, "improved" plans. While we pray that the new line-up of alliances against the terror emanating from Afghanistan will prove more effective than the old one, the new dangers of deals with the likes of Iran and (irony of ironies) Russia are undoubtedly formidable, though mostly unknown. What effect, for example, will our alliance with the other hated (erstwhile) superpower have on radical Muslim recruitment? Is it even conceivable that Iran is interested in helping reduce the risk of terrorist attacks on the United States, when they still call us the Great Satan? Or are we just helping them retain status for their more fundamentalist Shiite terrorists, who have been eclipsed in the terror pantheon in recent years, first by Saddam's more secular Sunnis, and now by bin Laden, whose roots are in the "puritanical Wahhabi sect of Sunni Muslims." [120]

Like many Americans, I have consumed dozens of articles in the three weeks since the attacks to try to gain a better understanding of the various sects, branches, ethnicities, histories, regimes and other divisions of the Muslim world, some part of which is now conducting a holy war against us. Only two things are clear to me at this point. First, the complexities are so mind-boggling that wading

---

[120] The New York Times article, "Bin Laden's Journey from Rich, Pious Boy To the Mask of Evil," September 30, 2001. See also the Wall Street Journal article, "Saudi Role in Alliance Fuels Religious Tension In Oil-Rich Kingdom," October 4, 2001. "According to Saudi dissident Saad al-Faqih, real action [by the Saudis to help the US] would break one of the 10 cardinal rules of Wahhabism, under which supporting a non-Muslim against a Muslim is the equivalent of apostasy and deserves death."

in with a friend-or-foe approach is bound in the long run to fail, however necessary it may be to meet the immediate threat. Second, the greatest danger to the United States now is that our actions will give those diverse Muslims a common enemy to unite against. Unfortunately, our coalition building is just the kind of policy that will lock us in to long term alliances engaged in that impossible planning task. And it is also just the kind of intervention that cannot help but convince wavering Muslims that they *should* unite against us. Just as it is not possible to dispense fairness domestically without igniting the *war of all against all*, giving out various measures of aid, trade, sanctions, etc, or asking different levels of support for our efforts of different countries is bound to generate resentment, animosity and unity among our enemies. It would be far safer and more effective to defend ourselves unilaterally and to seek as soon as possible to end the interventionism that is creating this threat to America.

The coalition building we are now engaged in is a continuation and intensification of that undertaken under the administration of the current President Bush's father, President George H. W. Bush. It was not surprising, of course, when the first President Bush was faced with the Iraqi invasion of Kuwait, that he put together the "Persian Gulf Coalition" to provide political cover for our military response to Saddam. Given his background as a former US ambassador to the UN, and the political capital he had invested in his signature policy of a "New World Order," his instincts were always to seek international consensus, rather than engage in unilateral action. The idea was that, in a sole superpower world, a principled US should not unilaterally bully its way around, but should lead the march of civilization to democracy and freedom. Naturally, the United Nations was the primary vehicle through which the initiatives to forge the New World Order would be vetted and implemented.

While that all sounded good, the reality is that maintaining global coalitions centered around the UN's interventionist role is an impossible task. Just as there is no way to satisfactorily dispense "justice" (equality of outcome) domestically, there is no way to do so internationally, either. And attempting to do so can only incite anger, hatred and not just Hobbes's metaphorical *war of all against all*, but actual war. While the US Government has been losing legitimacy at home because of its redistributionist role, the UN has become hated the world over for the same reason. That we are aggressively pursuing this redistributionist policy, and are visibly aligning ourselves with the hated international organization that is its most powerful symbol, can only harm our interests and, at the extreme, doom our nation. We have tried repeatedly to impress Muslims with our good intentions in recent years by protecting them from oppression or worse, and giving them aid. But in country after country, from Saudia Arabia to Afghanistan and Bosnia, from Somalia to Kosovo and Macedonia, there is no evidence that our stature has risen and much that it has fallen in Muslim communities around the world *as a result* of these interventions. And although we are trying to use international consensus to avoid the impression of bullying, the effect is exactly the opposite. We tell them that freedom, democracy and capitalism are unassailable virtues for a society, and they send their suicide bombers to attack us. We tell them that the Koran does not allow suicide, killing of civilians or Jihad on foreign soil, and they say *who are you to tell us what the Koran says.*

We Americans – of all citizens of all countries – should know that socialism and redistribution are contrary to Liberty. Not only do our foreign aid, trade agreements and other US-taxpayer-funded interventions rob US citizens of freedom (because we must fund them and because our businesses are affected by them), but they are disruptive and offensive to the freedom of their intended beneficiaries, too. Given that these policies can only proceed at the expense of Liberty, we should have long since suspected that they are at the root of our international problems. It is now too late to undo much of the damage, and it will be difficult to extract ourselves from the peril in which our inattention to Liberty has placed us. But I believe it can be done. The Rule of Law Amendment proposed in the last chapter can be thought of as a guide to necessary action now. Its purpose, if you will recall, is to prevent an array of harmful policies by preventing Government from reshuffling economic or social outcomes, which is Government's primary or only means of implementing those policies. The amendment would ban, for example, US participation in the redistributionist exercises of the United Nations, as well as any and all restrictions on trade. Although it would take time to debate and pass the amendment – probably too much time, given our current predicament – it can serve as a useful filter to discover what policies should be implemented and which should be abandoned immediately. Some harmful policies, such as general antitrust, may have to await the amendment's passage to be eliminated. But others, because they present a clear and present danger to national survival now, could be repealed or dropped right away. UN-based coalition building is one of them. The United States can and should act aggressively to defend itself, either unilaterally or with the help of whatever mutual defense alliances it chooses to call upon, such as NATO. But the US should remove itself from the UN and remove the UN from its soil. This would be a clear signal to the world of two new policies: 1) The United States will not engage in any coercion of any peoples or countries and 2) The United States will move forcefully and swiftly to dispatch its enemies and any other threats to its citizens.

Homeland Defense

The outpouring of patriotism following the September 11th attack is heartening. As grief turns to anger, a unified resolve to again take risks in defense of freedom is taking hold. I see cause for some optimism in this development, in spite of my fear described earlier that America will have great difficulty reviving the fervor and clarity of our Founders' devotion to freedom. But if we really do have the will now to endure disruption to our routines at home, if we do have the political courage to demand that our allies help us and that our enemies back off, if we have the will to use our military might against those who refuse, and the vision to reshape our intelligence services to meet the new threat – then, just perhaps, this same unity of purpose could be used to muster support for a return to freedom as our Founders saw it. I hope so, because not only is doing so necessary to prevent the economic, social and cultural decline of America, but it is now also necessary to defuse the terrorist threat and to defend ourselves against it. In fact, failure to do so will weaken us quickly and drastically, while generating animosity among and uniting our enemies. Moreover, if we cannot sustain our will to act in self defense – which it will prove impossible to do with a UN-based coalition approach – it is only a matter of time before our enemies will overwhelm us.

In the last chapter I despaired of the chances of repealing, piecemeal or otherwise, the antitrust laws that are so damaging to our infrastructure and freedom. While I still think repeal would be exceedingly difficult, and that going over the heads of the trustbusters via the Rule of Law Amendment is the best permanent solution, I find myself now suddenly hoping that emergency measures to repeal certain of the most critical segments of antitrust could be considered on national defense grounds. If, after all, we have the political will to immediately begin bailouts of the airlines with billions of dollars that will only perpetuate their problems, then surely that same will could be turned to the task of giving them a permanent antitrust exemption. Such an exemption would immediately energize capital to the task of consolidating the airlines, simultaneously solving their profitability problems, their coordination problems, their security problems and their inconvenience problems. Moreover, an airlines antitrust exemption would save those otherwise wasted billions for such critical needs as quickly building up and reshaping our defense and intelligence infrastructures to meet the needs of war in the age of terrorism.

Similarly, if we have the will to unite the world against terrorism, we just may have the will to restore freedom to our energy industry. Ever since the breakup of Rockefeller's Standard Oil, antitrust and related economic and political policies have forced us step by step to become reliant on foreign oil. We could immediately begin to address that vulnerability by providing an antitrust exemption for the energy industry. Not only would this quickly address the infrastructure problems described in this book, but we could hope before long to also remove the perennial concern over Mideast Oil and OPEC that have boxed us in politically to many interventions we could have done without. That our position in that corner of the world is based so much on inter-government relations rather than the simple commercial pursuits of free capitalists is the source of much tension and animosity. Not only would an antitrust exemption for the energy industry begin to relax such tensions, but it would quickly restore efficiency to a currently crippled piece of our infrastructure that, now that we are at war, we cannot afford to do without.

This is not the time or place to rehearse, industry by industry, the value of antitrust exemptions. Since the devastation wreaked by antitrust has been described earlier in this book, I think the reader can readily surmise why I still recommend exemptions or repeal or any other means of getting rid of this millstone. Indeed, I hope it is already obvious why my recommendation remains and that it remains not in spite of the fact that we are at war, but because we are at war. I hope it is also obvious why I believe it is now critical to repeal race- or religion-conscious laws. We cannot afford the group-versus-group animosity fostered by hate crime laws, affirmative action and other group-identity-based policies any more than we can afford to dawdle with inefficient industries. We just cannot afford to fan the flames of religious or racial hatred when their most likely victims today will be Arabs and Muslims whose victimization will recruit more terrorists. [121] We simply must go back to punishing the murderer because he murdered, not because he had a bad attitude toward his victim. To waste our time or money on socialist bailouts or bias crimes would be foolish now even if the results were not counterproductive to the intended purposes of these policies. Capitalism is really so simple. People can pursue their interests without interference by Government, and protected by Government from being assaulted or killed. We have no time now for anything else.

---

[121] According to FBI Director Robert Mueller on CNN on September 27 thirty FBI field offices had already opened a total of ninety hate crime investigations of alleged attacks on people that were (or were thought by their attackers to be) Arabs or Muslims.